CUC96
Component-Based Software Engineering

Managing Object Technology Series

Charles F. Bowman
Series Editor
President
SoftWright Solutions
Suffern, New York

CUC96

Component-Based Software Engineering

Collected and Introduced by

Thomas Jell

PUBLISHED BY THE PRESS SYNDICATE OF THE UNIVERSITY OF CAMBRIDGE
The Pitt Building, Trumpington Street, Cambridge CB2 1RP, United Kingdom

CAMBRIDGE UNIVERSITY PRESS
The Edinburgh Building, Cambridge CB2 2RU, UK
40 West 20th Street, New York, NY 10011-4211, USA
10 Stamford Road, Oakleigh, Melbourne 3166, Australia

http://www.cup.cam.ac.uk
http://www.cup.org

Published in association with SIGS Books & Multimedia

First published in 1998

Composition by Culligan & Co.

Printed in the United States of America

A catalog record for this book is available from the British Library

Library of Congress Cataloging-in-Publication Data is available.

ISBN 0-521-64821-1 paperback

Table of Contents

1. About the Conference

The First Component Users Conference

The very first Component User's Conference focused on today's most promising technology and took place at the Forum (Penta) Hotel, Munich Germany, July 15–July 19, 1996. With up to four parallel sessions, several excellent keynotes, exhibition and product presentations, over 40 speakers from all of the "hot spots" in today's componentware technology, plus over 150 attendees, the conference was a great success. It's remarkable that the first componentware conference was held in Europe and not, as usual, in the US or UK. So this time we'll have a US partner conference!

The conference provided a forum for thesentation and exchange of current work on various topics in componentware technology including, but not limited to, the following areas:

- Componentware platforms and services
- Methods for component design and architecture
- Development tools and environments
- Componentware languages
- Distributed object computing
- Formal component specifications
- Semantic descriptions for components
- Nonfunctional requirements (realtime, fault tolerance, reliability, etc.) for components and systems
- Patterns and frameworks

- Compound documents
- Interoperability
- Debugging and testing
- Industrial applications
- Integration of legacy systems

The conference included two Component-Ware Consortium days, when leading companies in that consortium presented their work and solutions. Numerous tutorials provided well-founded introductions into componentware and detailed informations about the new technologies. Component users and component providers found many opportunities to share their experiences and to discuss problems in depth. Executives found a great variety of information about current standards and future trends.

Web Sites for the Conference

The overall information as well as details about the conference can be found at www.geocities.com/SiliconValley/2121

For additional information, questions or the preliminary call for papers for the Second Component User's Conference 1997, send an email to:
Thomas.Jell@mchp.siemens.de
Michael.Klug@mchp.siemens.de

Organization

General Chair
Tom Jell, Siemens AG

Program Chair
Michael Klug, Siemens AG

US Vice Chair
David Smyth, Jet Propulsion Labs, NASA

Workshops Chair
Michael Stal, Siemens AG

Program Committee
Christian Ammon, Siemens Nixdorf
        Informationssysteme
Sean Baker, IONA Technologies
Prof. Ken Birman, Cornell University
Dr. Walter Bischofberger, UBILAB
Frank Buschmann, Siemens AG
Brian K. Cottman, I-Kinetics Inc.
Erich Gamma, IFA Unternehmensberatung
Michael Klug, Siemens AG
Prof. Pomberger, Universitaet Linz
Prof. Doug Schmidt, University of Washington
David Smyth, Jet Propulsion Labs, NASA
Michael Stal, Siemens AG

Local Arrangements Chair
Robert Nahm, Siemens AG

Conference Sponsors

ComponentWare® Consortium
I-Kinetics
IBM
Interactive Objects Siemens
SIGS

Acknowledgments

Special thanks go to all the people who worked hard to make the conference happen. Thanks especially to all the authors, speakers, exhibitors, participants, and, last but not least, all the organization team…and see you next year at CUC '97.

—Tom Jell

2. Speakers

Ping Bai

Ping Bai is a software engineer at Hughes Aircraft of Canada. Her interests include software development and reuse.

Frank Buschmann

Frank Buschmann is software engineer at Siemens Corporate Research and Development in Munich, Germany. His research interests are object technology and software architecture, specifically frameworks and patterns. He is project leader of a research project on patterns and is coauthor of the book *Pattern-Oriented Software Architecture—A System of Patterns* with Regine Meunier, Hans Rohnert, Peter Sommerlad, and Michael Stal. He is also a regular columnist on patterns for *OBJEKTspektrum* and *Object Expert*.

Paul Clements

Paul Clements is a senior researcher in MSI Research Institute, Loughborough University; previously he was a lecturer in Information Technology at Leicester Polytechnic. His current interests are primarily in the area of how to create and maintain flexible, configurable manufacturing systems.

Brian K. Cottman

http://www.componentware.com

Brian K. Cottman is Director of Marketing for I-Kinetics, the leading provider of component software and solutions for large systems. Mr. Cottman manages the overall product direction for I-Kinetics component products and services. He is also the visionary behind the founding of the ComponentWare Consortium, with the primary goal of making component software a reality via technical and business partnerships between users and vendors. He is active in the component software speaker circuit and has held technical positions with Electronic Data Systems, US West, and Cap Gemini. Mr. Cottman graduated Summa Cum Laude in 1989 with a Bachelor of Science degree in Finance and a minor in Economics.

Bruce H. Cottman

http://www.componentware.com

Bruce H. Cottman founded I-Kinetics in 1991 to provide software and consulting for object-based distributed systems. He has been involved with distributed systems research and development for over fifteen years. Previous positions include research staff at MIT and Lincoln Laboratory; Product Architect, Thomson Financial Network, Inc.; and founder and Vice President of R&D, Symbiotics, Inc. He currently serves as Chairman of the ComponentWare Consortium.

Dr. Cottman's primary responsibility is directing I-Kinetics as a leading consultant and software manufacturer for evolving legacy systems into component-based distributed systems. Dr. Cottman holds Bachelor of Science (1979) and Master of Science (1982) degrees in physics from MIT and a PhD (1985) in Physics from RPI.

Bernhard Hollunder

hollunder@io.freinet.de

Dr. Bernhard Hollunder is a consultant at Interactive Objects Software GmbH, a professional services organization specializing in distributed object systems. Hollunder is mainly interested in applying both the CORBA and componentware technologies.

Hermann Ilmberger

Hermann Ilmberger is a software engineer at Siemens AG, Corporate R&D, Munich. He developed programming, visualization, and debugging tools for parallel and distributed systems. Currently his work focuses on the technology of mobile, cooperating software agents.

Jose De Jesus

Jose De Jesus has worked with the Internet and OOP languages for over seven years. He is the author of Borland Pascal With Objects 7.0, published in 1993 by MIS:Press. His Java tutorials on the Web have attracted thousands of readers, gaining him an excellent reputation for presenting complex topics simply. His latest book is *IBM's Official Guide to Java.*

Nickolas Makrygiannis

Nickolas Makrygiannis is a PhD candidate at the Department of Informatics at the School of Economics in Gothenburg University. He got his Licentiate diploma in information systems in 1993, with a licentiate thesis on dispersed information systems and has a lecturing and research assignment at Gothenburg University, Sweden. His research interests are mainly focused on systems structuring. Currently he is involved in SEMLA, a project that aims to set up a theoretical and methodological framework for industrial development of complex systems based on an architectural and infrastructural approach.

Robert Nahm

Robert Nahm is with Corporate Research and Development at Siemens AG. He is an expert in formal description techniques in the area of distributed systems. He took part at the International Telecommunication Union (ITU) for the standardization of Message Sequence Charts.

Young Park

Young Park is an assistant professor of computer science at the School of Computer Science at the University of Windsor. His research interests include functional languages and programming, semantics-based program analysis, programming methodology, and software reuse. He has been working on methods and tools for supporting software reuse in functional programming.

Cuno Pfister

Cuno Pfister is the Managing Director of Oberon Microsystems, Inc., in Zurich, Switzerland. He received a PhD in computer science in 1993 from the Swiss Federal Institute of Technology (ETH Zurich). Later that year he cofounded Oberon Microsystems, where he and Clemens Szyperski designed the Oberon/F component framework.

Jürgen Schmitz

Jürgen Schmitz is a software engineer at Siemens AG, Corporate R&D, Munich. After working on the development team of the BS2000 mainframe operating system, he was a member of the distributed systems group, focusing on microkernel architectures and fault-tolerant computing. Currently his interests are in the technology of mobile and cooperative software agents and their application.

Thomas Schnekenburger

Dr. Thomas Schnekenburger received received his Master of Science degree in computer science from the University of Stuttgart in 1989, and his PhD in computer science from the Technische Universität München in Munich,

Germany, in 1994. Currently he is employed in a cooperative project between TUM and Siemens AG, Munich. His research area is load distribution support for distributed applications and distributed object-oriented frameworks such as CORBA.

David E. Smyth
http://mpfwww.jpl.nasa.gov/~dsmyth
David E. Smyth is well known for discovering effective ways of using new technologies. His presentations have been well received in the United States, Europe, the Middle East, and Asia. He is currently project leader on three Web-based intranet information systems and a research project addressing highly reliable distributed computing. He has a Bachelor of Science in Computer Science from the University of California, Irvine, and two decades of software development experience.

Peter Sommerlad
Peter Sommerlad is a software engineer and researcher at Siemens AG, Corporate Research and Development, in Munich, Germany. He has been working on object-oriented software engineering tools and innovative approaches to software development incorporating frameworks. He is investigating the application of design patterns for domain-specific framework construction. He is coauthor of the book *Pattern-Oriented Software Architecture—A System of Patterns* with Frank Buschmann, Regine Meunier, Hans Rohnert, and Michael Stal.

Malgorzata Steinder
Malgorzata Steinder graduated from the Computer Science Department, University of Mining and Metallurgy, in 1994. Her Master's thesis concerned mathematical models describing performance in the ATM network. Currently, she works as a research and teaching assistant in the Computer Science Department, UMM

Cracow. She is working on her PhD thesis and is interested in interoperability and trading in distributed processing.

Clemens Szyperski
Clemens Szyperski is an associate professor in the School of Computing Science and Director of the Research Concentration in Programming Languages and Systems, Queensland University of Technology, Brisbane, Australia. In 1992/93 he held a postdoctoral research science position at the International Computer Science Institute affiliated with the University of California at Berkeley. He received a PhD in computer science in 1992 from the Swiss Federal Institute of Technology (ETH Zurich) and a Dipl.-Ing. in EECE from the Aachen Institute of Technology (RTWH), Germany, in 1987.

In 1993 he cofounded Oberon microsystems, Inc., and codesigned the Oberon/F component framework, which is largely based on his PhD research. His research interests are extensible, component-oriented, and distributed systems and the programming languages to support them. He has participated in the Oberon and Ethos language and system projects at ETH, as well as in the Sather language and Tenet realtime communication projects at ICSI. At QUT he is heading the Gardens project, aiming at a language and systems infrastructure for parallel computing across high-performance networks of workstations.

Sabine Thürmel
Sabine Thürmel is a software engineer at Siemens AG, Corporate R&D, Munich. Her work focuses on problem solutions and tools for parallel and distributed systems (e.g., those based on the technology of mobile, cooperating agents), and the elaboration of future trends in software and engineering.

Emily A. Vander Veer
emilyv@vnet.ibm.com
Emily A. Vander Veer has participated in the design, implementation, and management of object-oriented software development projects for nearly six years. Currently employed by IBM in Austin, Texas, Ms. Vander Veer has spent the last eighteen months evangelizing OpenDoc and related object technologies.

Bernhard Wagner
Bernhard Wagner is a PhD student and research assistant at the Multimedia Laboratory of the University of Zurich. His research interests include object-oriented frameworks, multimedia authoring, and music. He is involved in the MET++ project, a class library for the development of multimedia applications. Based on MET++, a Web-browser with plug-ins for dynamic Web pages using composition of components has been awarded by BYTE at CeBIT '96.

Krzysztof Zieliński
Krzysztof Zieliński is a professor of computer science at the Computer Science Department, University of Mining and Metallurgy. He spent two years (1988–1990) in the Cambridge Olivetti Research Lab, where he worked on the first prototype of the ATM network. He is currently the main designer of the Cracow ATM MAN. He is also the Technical Manager of the Copernicus TOCOOS project and has authored approximately 100 publications.

3. Abstracts

David E. Smyth http://mpfwww.jpl.nasa.gov/ ~dsmyth: **Faster, Better, and Cheaper at JPL** Spacecraft projects require extremely distributed systems: The Mars Pathfinder project includes two nodes on Mars (the lander and the robotic rover), as well as hundreds of computing nodes on several LANS, and other clients and servers globally distributed across the Internet.

Emily A. Vander Veer: **Delivering the Benefits of Component Software: JavaScript and Related Component Technologies** It is predicted that by the year 2000, over 90% of the top 1000 companies worldwide will be exploiting the business opportunities provided by component-based Internet tools such as JavaScript. JavaScript is the most accessible of the new Internet tools. It allows nonprogrammers to build the most popular Internet application, a World Wide Web page, quickly and easily. It can also be integrated with other tools and component-based languages such as Java, OpenDoc, and CGI, enabling developers with more technical skills to build robust, interactive Web applications that exploit both component technology and legacy systems.

Brian K. Cottmann and Bruce H. Cottmann: **ComponentWare® Consortium Technology Plan White Paper** What is going on in the component software marketplace? Who is doing the research? What are some of the big projects? What industry alliances are being formed? The ComponentWare® Consortium has the answers to all of these questions because it is involved with all of the major industry players and users. The paper addresses the overall state of the market and current major research and client projects.

Young Park and Ping Bai: **Retrieving Software Components by Execution** The building-block approach to software reuse typically involves the process of identifying and retrieving from the reusable component repository existing components that potentially solve a specific problem. In this paper we present an execution-based method of retrieving reusable code components in a large reuse library to support more effective reuse in functional programming. The method is based on executing the code components on input samples that are generated systematically rather than using randomly generated samples or samples provided by the user. The input samples are generated based on program reasoning techniques, such as various inductions; one sample is provided for the base case and two for the inductive step. The proposed retrieval is incorporated into a prototype software base system for reuse called WiSeR.

Malgorzata Steinder and Krzysztof Zieliński: **Service Location in Multi-ORB Distributed Systems** The main subject addressed is service location and crossing referencing domains in a multiORB environment subdivided into technical and administrative domains. We propose an architecture that allows a client to find and establish a connection with a server in another domain. We present components of this architecture, their structure and functionality, and methods of cooperation with trading and naming services that are available in particular domains. The main focus is on interoperability aspects: design and function of inter-ORB cooperation modules and object reference mapping.

Bernhard Wagner, Ian Sluijmers, Dominik Eichelberg, and Philipp Ackerman: Black-Box Reuse within Frameworks Based on Visual Programming

MET++ is a fully object-oriented application framework that supports spatial and temporal composition of text, 2-D, 3-D graphics, video, audio, and music. The public-domain MET++ class library, which is based on ET++, allows prototyping and rapid development of seamlessly integrated multimedia applications. The classes offered within MET++ are most easily reused in a black-box manner, since only the interface and not the internals of a class have to be understood by the programmer. We took black-box reuse a step further by allowing visual composition of components (i.e., without programming or scripting). This visual environment offers an easy access to the composition of executable multimedia documents.

Thomas Schnekenburger: Automatic Load Distribution for CORBA Applications

Load distribution is a classical problem in distributed systems. Load distribution has to assign particular entities to particular targets so that given performance requirements are met. Load distribution for CORBA environments is still a research topic. Until now, the application programmer has to manually assign entities to targets. This paper surveys common methods for load distribution and discusses their applicability to CORBA environments. Furthermore, a general model describing all possible levels for load distribution in CORBA is introduced.

Hermann Ilmberger, Jürgen Schmitz, and Sabine Thürmel: Mobile Agents—Mobile Components

Mobile agents are software components that autonomously fulfill tasks in a distributed system by moving between several computers, taking with them their program code and accumulated execution state. The basic motivation for mobility is to bring the data processing program as near as possible to the processed data. It may be cheaper to move a small or medium-grain agent to a server where the data is located than it is to transfer back and forth many requests to the data over a possibly slow network. This paper elaborates on the relation of mobile agents to components, gives an overview of existing mobile agent systems and application scenarios, and describes the swarm intelligence technology: cooperating mobile agents for adaptive problem solutions.

Nickolas Makrygiannis: Toward Mass-Customized Information Systems

For a long time we have experienced a shift from customer-specific development to mass production of information systems. It is popular to think in "LEGO" terms, or to use the car industry as a metaphor for how information systems (IS) should be built based on a set of predefined system blocks. However, information systems are neither cars nor LEGO spacecrafts. They can be used to rearrange work settings and communication patterns and thereby organizational structure. They provide users with alternative ways to cooperate that lead to new needs and requirements. To meet new demands, IS structures must be flexible. That flexibility should leaven the whole systems development philosophy, not just the final IS product. Therefore, we need to enlarge existing IS development methodology with methods and tools for mass customizing IS. This paper is a theoretical contribution to the debate on systems structuring, wherein organizational aspects are represented as well as their technical counterparts. A number of research efforts are presented, which could prepare us to deal with mass customization of IS.

John Edwards, Paul Clements, Jack Gascoigne, and Ian Coutts: Component-Based Systems: The Basis of Future Manufacturing Systems

In order to achieve and maintain world-class status, manufacturing enterprises are increasingly required to reengineer their businesses to maximise efficiency and agility. To enable enterprises to successfully achieve this process, a radical change is required in the software systems that underpin modern enterprises. Clearly there is a requirement to move from large, monolithic pieces of software to finer-grain component software or business objects. This paper reports on some of the early ideas proposed by researchers at the MSI Research Institute for creating and supporting manufacturing systems using component technology.

Robert Nahm: Designing and Documenting Componentware with Message Sequence Charts

Component-based software technology builds applications from single, black-box software components. The challenge is the smooth integration of components into a homogenous application. The integration of components depends on the description of interfaces. Currently, interfaces are described by the signature of operations, but these do not contain any semantic information about how to use operations. For this problem, a scenario-based language like Message Sequence Chart can help. Message Sequence Chart, which can be compared to Use Cases and Interaction Diagrams, is a graphical language, used mostly in the area of telecommunication systems, that describes traces of distributed systems. The talk gives an introduction to the language and shows how to desribe and document black-box components such that the integration of components is easier.

Robert H. High, Jr.: Component Model for Managed Objects in Large-Scale Distributed Systems

In this paper, we introduce a component framework for business objects. With that as a foundation, we then describe how components can he assembled along with object management mix-in classes to form a managed object. We discuss the effects of object granularity on object management. We demonstrate the use of aggregation in determining where objects are created, and in assigning objects names, security, and enterprise policy. Finally, we discuss some of the technical problems and solutions that are introduced by aggregation.

Frank Buschmann and Peter Sommerlad: What Is a Pattern?

The objective of this tutorial is to present a new way of thinking about software architecture, one that focuses on patterns and their practical use in software development. First, we give an explanation on the notion of patterns. We then present several important patterns relevant for componentware, distributed systems, and graphical user interfaces. Each of them gives a solution schema to a recurring design problem in software development. A pattern comes with a description of the context, where applicable; the problem it addresses; the solution, with its structure and dynamics; and a guide to its concrete implementation in software.

Cuno Pfister and Clemens Szyperski: Why Objects Are Not Enough

Today, the beginning of a shift from object-oriented programming to component-oriented programming can be observed. Component-oriented programming provides better support for whole collections of objects, for dynamic loading of classes, and for safety, and it allows better decoupling between components than does object-oriented programming. Frameworks follow this trend by shifting support away from traditional closed applications to truly modular, open component assemblies.

Cuno Pfister and Clemens Szyperski: Oberon/F: A Cross-Platform Component-Oriented Framework

Today, the beginning of a shift from object-oriented programming to component-oriented programming can be observed. Component-oriented programming provides better support for whole collections of objects, for dynamic loading of classes, and for safety, and it allows better decoupling between components than does object-oriented programming. Frameworks follow this trend by shifting support away from traditional closed applications to truly modular, open component assemblies. Oberon/F is a horizontal framework that currently runs under Windows 3.1/95/NT and Mac OS. It was designed along component-oriented programming principles to support the run-time integration of independently developed components. It's compound document architecture abstracts away the differences between OLE2 and OpenDoc containers, and thus makes components easier to implement independent of the particular underlying component software technology.

Jose De Jesus: Let's Brew Some Java

Java is undeniably giving the Web a caffeine boost! Don't wait any longer to become part of the Java development community. The author of *IBM's Official Guide to Java* addresses the fundamentals of Java programming, covering Java's OOP model, applications, and applets. The difference between Java and JavaScript are also discussed, as is Java's relation to CORBA/DSOM, OpenDoc, and OLE.

Bernhard Hollunder: Specification and Implementation of CORBAservices A Case Study—Extended Abstract

While the specification of an Object Request Broker (ORB) defines basic functions for the transparent invocation of requests in a heterogeneous distributed environment, the so-called CORBAservices specify further sets of fundamental services that greatly facilitate the realization of distributed systems. The deployment of the standard operations provided by CORBAservices not only simplifies the development of large-scale systems, but also enables the building of programs that are easily portable between the ORB implementations of different vendors. One specific service—event management—is discussed in detail.

Sverker Norrefeldt: GINA: An Object-Oriented Run-Time and Development Solution for Distributed Object Computing

This paper describes Siemens Nixdorf's GINA (General Interface for Network Applications), a framework for the implementation and operation of object-oriented transaction-based client-server applications.

4. Papers

Faster, Better, and Cheaper at JPL

David E. Smyth
http://mpfwww.jpl.nasa.gov/~dsmyth

Overview

- *Object decomposition:* Responsibility, knowledge, collaborations, and the Law of Demeter

- *Distributed state:* Omniscience is impossible and unnecessary

- *Transfer of control:* Asynchronous message passing (or get another job)

- *Brittle vs. robust:* Not an easy tradeoff

- *Development process:* It beats herding cats

Introduction

Spacecraft projects require extremely distributed systems: The Mars Pathfinder project includes two nodes on Mars (the lander and the robotic rover), as well as hundreds of computing nodes on several LANS, and other clients and servers globally distributed across the Internet.

Technical challenges include critical communications links that are slow, potentially noisy, and unreliable, with severe delays (sometimes days between packet handshake completion); klunky legacy systems that are complex, expensive, sophisticated, and essential; critical, sophisticated software behaviors that cannot be tested before launch; extremely high cost of failure; and absolutely fixed schedules and budgets.

The distributed software system for Mars Pathfinder is collectively called the End-to-End Information System (EEIS). Subsystems include commercial off-the-shelf packages, JPL-developed legacy systems, and newly developed code. The more recently developed code tends to be more object oriented than the older code. All software developed by the Pathfinder project is object oriented.

"The purpose of a position paper is to provide a seed for debate and discussion." This is a position paper! The expressed opinions are entirely those of the author and should in no way be construed to represent the opinions of any organization or person. The author may change his opinions at any time.

Object Decomposition

In this decade, everyone is developing object-oriented software, and for good reason.

Less well understood and agreed-upon are techniques for identifying objects in the problem domain and mapping them into objects in the solution (software) domain. Parallel and distributed systems introduce additional concerns: Where, on which computing node (or nodes), do the various objects exist?

In the first months of the Pathfinder project, significant time and effort was expended to try and ensure we would "do the right things." The entire software team spent the first 25% of the development schedule on learning and teaching. The object-oriented software development experience of the team members varied from none to since Simula. Books by Wirfs-Brock, Booch, Coad/Yourdon, and Rumbaugh were studied. Innumerable papers and articles were read and discussed. Amazingly, no physical violence erupted.

The most significant result of this effort was a reasonably consistent vocabulary, in words and ideas, across the team members. Also, general guidelines were identified and agreed upon.

As is usual in software-development efforts, these guidelines were not enforced and were inconsistently applied. (Programmers do tend to be rather individualistic. Which is a good thing: It provides yet more data on what works and what doesn't.)

Object Decomposition: Responsibility

The first and most widely adhered-to tenet was to divide the problem along lines of responsibility. This is different from the original object identification technique of "find the nouns in the problem statement." Personally, I felt reluctance towards this concept at first, because it sounded too much like functional decomposition, which we all know doesn't work as well as "find the nouns."

Nevertheless, the value of this concept was immense. Early on, it became clear that code that strongly adhered to this principle had substantially narrower interfaces than did code that paid less heed. Most commonly, "responsible" objects never needed to return status values to collaborators—the object was responsible for both nominal and off-nominal behavior. Just like in real life!

As the system progressed, other advantages became apparent: It was far easier to apply the other guidelines if this first guideline was obeyed.

Object Decomposition: Knowledge

This concept is more significant than we initially thought. With a distributed system, the distribution of knowledge has a significant impact on performance, capability, and robustness. Any object-oriented design tends

to have the data where it is needed, hence our minor emphasis on this concept—why worry about it, when it just happens more-or-less the right way? Our bandwidth constraints between the nodes on Mars and Earth are so severe that more intelligent distribution of objects may provide a more efficient system.

When the Pathfinder EEIS is evolved to support the next Mars mission and other deep space missions later this year, this issue will be addressed in more detail.

Object Decomposition: Collaborations

Collaborations are the reason for interobject communications. Therefore, the existence of collaborative relationships is an important factor in determining where distributed and parallel objects should exist—which threads, processes, processors, nodes, and/or networks.

Object Decomposition and The Law...

... of Demeter, of course. Demeter is a genius, and should probably get the Nobel Prize. See "Contributions to teaching object-oriented design and programming" by Karl J. Lieberherr and Arthur J Riel, OOPSLA '89 as ACM SIGPLAN 24,11 (Nov '89), 11–22. The Law can be paraphrased as, "Any method must operate only on the object's existing state and the arguments to the method; no data shall be required from any other source during the execution of a method."

Note two things: First, the Law implies that no method shall return any value (otherwise the caller cannot obey the Law). Second, the Law is really just a description of dataflow processing in the context of objects.

The wonderful thing about following this Law is that the result is a set of objects that can be multithreaded and distributed. Temporal coupling and synchronization is eliminated, avoiding three of the nastiest problems in real-time and distributed systems: critical sections, priority inversions, and deadlock.

We have observed that obeying the Law of Demeter is quite easy and nonintrusive if and only if the Law is in the forefront of one's consciousness throughout the development effort. It is very hard to transform existing code so that it complies with the Law.

Law-Breaking Servers

It is always possible to transform software or to encapsulate legacy software so that it obeys the Law of Demeter. However, there are situations, specifically involving servers, where it is very tempting to break the Law. We can classify collaborations between servers and clients in these ways:

- The client almost always needs the data for frequent behaviors.

- The rate of change of the server's data is slower to about the same degree as the rate of activity of the client: Obey Law.

- The rate of change of the server's data is faster (e.g., system clock) than the rate of activity of the client: Maybe Break Law.

- The client almost never needs the information.

- The server's data is cheap and slowly changing with respect to the activity of the client: Obey Law.

- The server's data is expensive or rapidly changing with respect to the activity of the client: Maybe Break Law.

It is important to mention that is it still not necessary to break the Law in the above cases, but it can be tempting. It is essential to remain aware of the significant costs associated with breaking the Law:

- There can be serious performance penalties if the objects are not running on the same machine, in the same lightweight process.

- Running objects with radically differing responsibilities within the same lightweight process and/or on the same machine can increase integration and maintenance costs, as bugs can be masked and symptoms confused.

- Redundancy is no longer transparent and is much more difficult and error prone; therefore, fault tolerance can be seriously compromised.

Responsibility-driven decomposition, combined with the Law of Demeter, allowed us to deliver our real-time, distributed system under absolutely strict cost and schedule constraints, with no unpaid overtime and with very little paid overtime (much less than 10%).

Distributed State: Omnisience is Impossible—and Unneccesary

The Universe is asynchronous, without any absolute truths: Everything is relative. This is true at all scales—relativity is essential to understanding Galaxies, an elevator, and quarks.

Therefore, who in Hell came up with the idea of centralized databases? Shoot that person before they do any more damage!

Smileys should be inserted by the reader ;-)

Just as nature provides us with the concept of object orientation, nature can also provide us with clues to solving distributed state problems. Relativity, specifically: Objects can share state based on location and rate (execution), not on time, because there is no concept of absolute time. Therefore, synchronization is bogus.

Luckily, both responsibility and Demeter help out here again. An object is responsible for something, based on what it knows at the time it's asked to do it. Just like real life!

I wish I came up with this idea, but references include the paper by C.E. Hewitt and H. Baker entitled "Laws for Communicating Parallel Processes" in the August 1977 IFIP Congress Proceedings.

Transfer of Control: Asynchronous Message Passing...

...or get another job. Because synchronization is impossible, using blocking-transfer-of-control mechanisms is obviously inappropriate. I feel very strongly about this, but YMMV.

Our experience on Mars Pathfinder is that the software that uses message passing is better than the software which does not: The message-based code is much more compact for a given amount of capability; the message-based code gets delivered sooner with fewer bugs and significantly less integration problems. This could also be a reflection of the experience of the developers—those with more experience are more apt to use messages than those with less experience; those with more experience generate more reliable code sooner than those with less experience.

There is no free lunch, however. The architects and programmers must be aware of the significance of state transitions. In the beginning, we intended to use the Actor model for our objects. One of the key characteristics of Actor is the explicit specification that the set of behaviors (methods) of an object is a function of the object (instance) state.

If an object can always accept all methods, in any order, then it can be considered "stateless," and therefore the set of methods is constant. Many programming languages support only this kind of object. Many books mention only such objects.

However, we find that there are many situations where it is impossible, or at least very impractical, to make a "stateless" object. We have software objects that control hardware devices. Some actions performed by the hardware take a very long time (we can compute millions of instructions before the hardware is finished with an action).

Here is a specific example: One of the components necessary for transmitting from the spacecraft to Earth is called the Telemetry Modulation Unit (TMU). There is a software object that is responsible for monitoring and controlling the TMU hardware.

The TMU hardware is monitored and controlled via memory-mapped registers. The TMU is off most of the time; we only turn it on a few times per week when we are going to transmit. When the TMU is off, the CPU must not access (read nor write) the memory-mapped register addresses, otherwise the processor will halt and eventually reboot.

It takes up to several seconds to turn on the TMU. When the TMU is powered on, it comes up in an operative but ineffective configuration—we always need to configure after it is powered up. There are many ways in which the TMU will be configured during the mission, based on mission phase, spacecraft fault conditions, and so on. Therefore, the TMU object does not autonomously configure the hardware, but rather configures the hardware according to commands from other on-board software or according to commands within scripts uplinked from the human operators on Earth.

Clearly, the behavior of the TMU software object depends on the state of the hardware. And, clearly, some of the hardware state transitions take a long time—much too long to make a client block until the TMU is turned on before allowing commands that configure the TMU. Also, it may be convenient to decouple the commands that power on the TMU from commands that configure the TMU—we will know the schedule for communication windows, and these will stay quite constant, but some configurations of the TMU may need to be changed to recover from on-board fault conditions.

There are at least these three ways of dealing with objects that have slow state transitions:

- Block the client(s) until the state transition is complete. This is easy to implement, but a very bad idea: It causes the interface to the object to be very broad (the client must consider the state of the object and invoke methods in a specific order); it causes the dynamic behavior of clients to be intimately linked to the state of the server.

- Maintain information within the object that will be used at some time in the future, when the slow state transition is completed. Perhaps this can be considered a predictive state of the object. Deceptively easy to implement, but a maintenance nightmare. This is a real hack.

- Incoming messages are enqueued, and the receiver scans the queue rather than simply operating on the first message in the queue. This eliminates the problems of the above approaches, but introduces the problem that messages are no longer processed in order. If the receiver is a responsible object, then this is usually not a problem, but I don't know how to prove that this is never a problem.

Brittle vs. Robust

This is a surprisingly difficult tradeoff. My experience has been that it is best and easiest to start out with a brittle system: assert( ) all

over the place, reboot when there is a problem. This allows the software to develop within well known and thoroughly enforced constraints on the software state. Problems are noticed as soon as possible. Testing is much easier, because far fewer software states are possible.

As the software becomes more mature (when something like 95% of the capabilities are delivered), then the system can be made more robust.

Again, responsibility and the Law contribute to making this maturation easy: The responsible object attempts to carry on, working with incomplete or somewhat inconsistent state. Since the "caller" never sees a return value, the fact that the object succeeded where before it failed cannot be detected.

Downstream, of course, there is an effect. Therefore, the problems do not go away completely.

Development Models: It Beats Herding Cats

We can talk all day about this, and I intend to have some good stuff on this topic well before the workshop, published via the Web. This is already long enough ... but it's a good start.

David E. Smyth is well known for discovering effective ways of using new technologies. His presentations have been well received in all US time zones, Europe, the Middle East, and Asia. He is currently project lead on three different web-based intranet information systems, and a research project addressing highly reliable distributed computing. He has a BS in Computer Science from the University of California, Irvine, and two decades of software-development experience.

Delivering the Benefits of Component Software
JavaScript and Related Component Technologies

Emily A. Vander Veer
emilyv@vnet.ibm.com

Introduction

The worldwide number of Internet connections is estimated to be around 30 million, and the percentage increase is predicted by some to be as high as ten percent a month. In addition, the World Wide Web is currently growing faster than any other Internet protocol, at a rate that could triple in a year. A recent Consumer Online Services report predicts that 35.2 million households will be online in the year 2000, up from 9.6 million in 1995. The same report estimates that online industry revenues, which reached $2.2 billion in 1995, will top $14 billion by the year 2000. The staggering growth of Internet applications is a specialized case of the trend toward network-centric computing made possible by component software technology. Along with the Internet, the Intranet, or "internal Internet," is an increasingly attractive implementation choice. Using the same Web technologies as the Internet, the Intranet offers a more controlled environment for internal corporate applications.

This paper explores the benefits of using JavaScript in conjunction with other component technologies in several enterprise scenarios. Because Netscape Communication's JavaScript implementation is still evolving, and because even accurate implementation details are relatively meaningless without context, this paper will focus on the role of JavaScript in enterprise software systems rather than on technical specifications.

First, because JavaScript is a Web-development tool, we'll take a look at the overall benefits of deploying component-based applications via the Internet and the Intranet. Then we'll shift our focus to the enterprise and explore the role JavaScript can play in reengineering business applications such as sales, marketing, and customer service. Finally, we'll get a high-level overview of how JavaScript works and how it can interact with several other popular component-based technologies to create globally distributed, network-centric applications.

Component Software & the Internet

One of the newest and most accessible tools for creating Web pages, JavaScript is the most popular Internet application. JavaScript is an easy-to-use, object-based scripting language that allows users to create interactive Web applications capable of interfacing with other Internet-enabled components.

Component software is uniquely suited to Internet applications for several reasons. In general, components, because they lack the overhead associated with traditional monolithic applications, are relatively small. This compactness is an asset in terms of both storage (less to store means lower cost) and distribution (quicker transmission also translates to lower cost).

Also, since they are typically implemented by means of an object-oriented architecture, components distributed over the Internet have the distinct advantage of being easier to use than data files alone (the traditional approach), because of their encapsulation of data and function. An example of this advantage is that users who download object-based components don't need to buy additional software in order to use them. And when you're using the Internet as a vehicle for sales or customer service, the easier your applications are for a customer to use, the better.

Another benefit of component-based solutions, often discounted but of great practical use, is their ability to adapt to existing legacy systems. There is no need to rearchitect and re-implement a system to exploit the advantages of component software. Instead, components can be added to existing systems in an incremental fashion. An example of this is an application that presents a component-based client interface while it retains the security and reliability of existing mainframe data stores and logic. As with most things, component software is a tool that is most effective when used judiciously and appropriately.

Component Software & the Intranet

The term *Intranet* refers to distributed applications implemented on dispersed wide area networks (WANs), developed and used primarily by members of a single organization. These are typically corporate networks, and the goal of the applications is to share confidential information among an organization's employees.

Many of these applications can be developed and deployed using the same Web technologies that Internet applications use to provide user interface and data transfer. The benefits of Intranet development vs. Internet development are that in the case of Intranet development, developers can usually dictate a specific Web browser to be used. Since browser software varies widely in term of graphical and textual representation, level of HyperText Markup Language (HTML) support, and other factors, having all users standardized on the

same browser eliminates the need to develop multiple interfaces for multiple browser access. Maintaining secure data on an Intranet application is often easier, too, since the data servers are generally under the physical control of the corporation.

Component Software & the Enterprise

One advantage of component software is that it allows developers to plug together components from disparate systems. Whether or not a system is distributed internally or globally via the Internet, the focus must remain on the needs of the business. Only after a system has been designed conceptually is it appropriate to address implementation issues such as distribution of function, communication synchronicity, and performance.

JavaScript provides two distinct benefits based on whether the script is to run on a client or on a server:

- The ability to animate a Web page so that user interactions (mouse click, keyboard entry, etc.) trigger functions on a client (much like triggers in database forms builders)
- The ability to define functions that can access other programs running on a server

These characteristics make possible an astounding opportunity to reengineer business practices such as sales, marketing, personnel, and customer service. For example:

Sales
Commerce appears to be the Holy Grail of Internet communication. Imagine a Web page that allows visitors to peruse a catalog, make a selection, and enter payment information. Then imagine that the same application in-

vokes other components that can progressively:

- Access a financial institution to verify a potential customer's credit information

- Access the company mainframe to decrease inventory by the number of items purchased

- Forward the necessary details to the shipping department so that the order can be filled immediately

JavaScript, in concert with other tools and components, can make this scenario a reality. The deployment of such an application would likely be an addition to, rather than a replacement of, traditional sales channels. The result would be to expand the company's reach, make it easier for customers to make purchases without an increase in sales staff, and at the same time preserve transaction security and full integration with legacy systems.

Marketing

The first, and still the most prevalent, use of Web pages is for marketing. JavaScript lets users "punch up" Web pages to include graphics, animation, and sound. It also provides an easy way to gather marketing statistics, such as how many visitors click a button to get more information on a specific product.

In addition, JavaScript-enabled Web pages can provide visitors a customized experience based on interactive input. For example, if a visitor indicates that she is interested in making wholesale purchases, a different set of Web pages might be displayed than those available to a retail purchaser.

Imagine a marketing Web page created by a company whose business is creating and delivering customized presentations. In addition to traditional text-based information about the company and its services, the Web page could contain film clips and sound to demonstrate the quality of the company's work. It could also check a host database to see whether the visitor might be entitled to a special company rate or to refer the visitor to the Web sites of previously satisfied customers.

Personnel

Finding the right applicant to fill a position is no easy task. Since the number of Internet connections has exploded in the last few years, more potential candidates are online every day. Imagine a JavaScript-enabled Web page that not only describes a position but queries the applicant, accesses a rule-based reasoning component to assign probabilities for a match, and then stores the data on a server for further manipulation.

For some organizations such as the Federal Government or university systems, Internet-based human resource applications for existing employees might be appropriate. Changes in benefits and procedures could be communicated via a series of interactive Web pages that would be accessible to employees across the country, both at home and at work.

Customer Service

The difference between success and failure in today's service economy often rests on the quality of customer service. The freight industry has already begun tracking packages from door to door by requiring employees who come in contact with the shipments to enter location information into their tracking systems. Imagine a JavaScript-enabled Web page that allows customers to track their packages online from any machine connected to the Internet.

Another example might be a JavaScript-enabled banking application that allows customers to query loan rates, check balances, and transfer funds from anywhere in the world. Customers could do 90% of their banking from their home computer! Banks wouldn't need to staff as many branch offices, customer satisfaction would increase, and the cost of banking services would decrease.

JavaScript: How Does It Work?

Based on Netscape's association with Sun Microsystems and Sun's Java implementation, JavaScript (formerly called "LiveScript") was designed to provide the most useful subset of Web-page–building functions (for example, the ability to create and manipulate forms, buttons, and text elements) in a simple, straightforward language. Those who want more advanced features than simple calculations or event-driven responses can integrate their scripts with other component technologies. This gives JavaScript the flexibility and power of a complex language while allowing it to retain its ease of use.

An object-based scripting language designed to be used with HTML, JavaScript is currently supported by Navigator, Netscape's Web browser. Navigator commands at least three quarters of the Web browser market and is available for the Macintosh, Windows 3.1, Windows 95, Windows NT, and several flavors of UNIX. The JavaScript specification is also available for other companies to license and implement in their own products. Over two dozen industry-leading companies have expressed their endorsement of the JavaScript specification to date, so expect to see more JavaScript-enabled tools on the market in the near future. The support of all of these companies is an encouraging sign that JavaScript will eventually become an open standard, helping to bring the full benefit of component software to the market.

HTML, a text-based markup language that allows users to create graphical interfaces, was invented in 1989. By 1993, the Web had emerged as the most popular Internet tool, due in large part to the ease of creating and viewing Web pages with HTML. JavaScript continues this tradition of a compact tag language with a well-defined scope. JavaScript scripting statements are embedded into HTML to allow users to add dynamic function to existing Web pages without having to learn a full-blown development language.

Because JavaScript is object-based, a new user must become familiar with its (fairly small) object model in order to use it effectively. Many of the objects available in JavaScript are user interface objects: button, checkbox, date, string, document, frame, etc. JavaScript scripts typically define behaviors and then associate these behaviors to the objects available. For example, a JavaScript might define a function that checks to see if the text a user enters is alphabetic—if numbers exist, a warning message will be displayed. This function might then be attached to every text-entry field on a Web page so that when a viewer leaves each text-entry field the function executes.

Netscape Navigator's JavaScript implementation allows developers to see the JavaScript source underlying a Web page, save it, and print it. This is a quick way for new users to learn JavaScript by example; studying an existing script and tweaking it is often much quicker than creating one from scratch.

Of course, whether you're developing Internet or Intranet applications, distribution of function is an important consideration. In this respect, JavaScript is very useful on the client, enabling "intelligent" Web pages that gather and process visitor input. Once the data is gathered, it can then be streamed to remote programs via HTTP (HyperText Transfer Protocol) or CGI (Common Gateway Interface), which is described below.

But there's also a place for JavaScript on the server. Netscape's LiveWire JavaScript implementation brings the power of JavaScript's simple scripting interface to server applications. This is the "missing link" of Internet/Intranet enterprise solutions. With LiveWire's database connectivity, Web developers have more flexibility in terms of integrating legacy data into their Web applications.

JavaScript and Other Component Technologies

Because it was designed to be compact and easy to use, JavaScript represents a subset (albeit a comprehensive one) of function available to Web developers. JavaScript makes provision for more complex functions, however, via user exits to other programs and LiveWire's database connectivity. The tools below do not comprise a comprehensive list, but instead offer an example of the possibilities.

Java

Although the name sounds similar to JavaScript, Sun Microsystems' Java itself is very dissimilar. Unlike JavaScript, which is compact, interpreted, and loosely typed, Java is a complete, compiled, strongly typed object-oriented programming language. Compiled Java programs, called *applets,* are executable on several platforms.

These two technologies can collaborate, however. JavaScript scripts can interact with Java applets at run-time by getting and setting exposed properties of the applet (that is, passing information to the applet to customize its behavior).

LiveWire

Netscape's LiveWire is a set of tools designed to facilitate the creation and management of Web server applications. One of these tools is the version of JavaScript that facilitates database integration, thus enabling Web developers to implement data retrieval, processing, and

storage using standard relational database conventions such as SQL.

The following diagram shows the flow of information from the browser through the Web to a database application:

Browser → Web → Web Server → LiveWire → Database Client → Database Server

The flow of return data from the database back to the Web browser follows the same sequence, only in reverse:

Database Server → Database Client → LiveWire → Web Server → Web → Browser

You can think of LiveWire as server-side JavaScript. To date, JavaScript has been widely adopted as the standard scripting language for creating intelligent Web pages. With LiveWire, Netscape brings JavaScript to their Web server offerings, FastTrack and Enterprise.

CGI

CGI, or the Common Gateway Interface, permits interaction between Web client and host operating systems through HTTP. CGI gives JavaScript scripts the ability to make calls to programs (usually Perl scripts or C programs, because of the cross-platform availability of these tools) that run remotely on server machines. JavaScript can pass arguments to these programs as well as accept return information.

While CGI isn't properly classified as a component technology, it does represent the cables, if you will, that allow other components to plug into each other. Since CGI itself doesn't address such issues as communication synchronicity, two-way data exchange, or security, the CGI program must do this.

OpenDoc (Arabica)

OpenDoc/Java interoperability is currently being pursued by IBM, which recently demonstrated a prototype of Arabica, the first implementation of the Java Beans initiative. Arabica, which is based on OpenDoc technology, will provide an open, cross-platform component architecture for developing Java applets and applications. The purpose of the Java Beans initiative is to allow developers to write portable Java applets from reusable software components.

The combination of OpenDoc and Java is very powerful. From OpenDoc, Arabica gains the ability to structure Java applets that interoperate seamlessly to form complex applications. From Java, Arabica gains the ability to run cross-platform and to be scripted via JavaScript. Developers will be able to create Arabica components through any Java development environment, including the forthcoming VisualAge for Java from IBM.

Conclusion

JavaScript is an easy way to extend HTML and create dynamic, interactive Web pages. It also exemplifies the component software model by encouraging script reuse on the client and by supporting the integration of components developed with other tools, both on the client and on the server. While Netscape's implementation of JavaScript is proprietary, the JavaScript specification is available to the industry. Press announcements from several top compa-nies, including Apple, AT&T, IBM, Microsoft, and Oracle, indicate that JavaScript implementations will soon become an open standard.

JavaScript's ability to integrate with other component technologies gives it enormous flexibility. Think of it as a director in a movie production studio: it specifies which events trigger which actions, but it doesn't have to define precisely how those actions are carried out—that's up to the individual actors (Java applets, Perl scripts, and so on.)

JavaScript is a powerful addition to the arsenal of component-based application development tools. It's important to remember that although component software offers enterprises a way to reengineer business processes completely, an enterprise can choose to embrace this technology at any level. For those who choose an incremental approach, JavaScript offers an easy way to add client components to existing systems. As the decision is made to reengineer more of the legacy system, LiveWire JavaScript provides database integration at the server level to allow full distribution of application function.

Emily A. Vander Veer has participated in the design, implementation, and management of object-oriented software development projects for nearly six years. Currently employed by IBM in Austin, Texas, Ms. Vander Veer has spent the last eighteen months evangelizing OpenDoc and related object technologies. She can be reached at emilyv@vnet.ibm.com.

ComponentWare® Consortium Technology Plan White Paper

Brian K. Cottmann and Bruce H. Cottmann

Overview

The primary goal of the ComponentWare Consortium (CWC) technology plan is to overcome barriers to building and deploying mission-critical information systems by using verified, reusable software components (ComponentWare). The adoption of the ComponentWare infrastructure by developers and systems integrators is linked to the successful implementation of emerging, object-based, distributed computing frameworks—initially, CORBA and OLE/COM. Once the leading platform vendors have embraced these object-based frameworks, it is inevitable that users will also do so.

Object-based distributed computing frameworks, such as CORBA and OLE/COM, are generally classified as distributed object management systems (DOMS). The CWC technology plan leverages emerging DOMS and advances them by developing software components and services that are required for demanding, domain-specific, information and data-management systems. The CWC currently recognizes three levels of participation. *Technology Providers* will create the components and the underlying infrastructure. *Solution Providers* will plan and implement component-based solutions. *Strategic Partners* will use ComponentWare solutions in

such areas as: space-mission telemetry data management and analysis, turbine-engine design and engineering, logistics management, and capital market risk management.

The CWC technology plan also includes a ComponentWare system engineering methodology called the Information Factory Methodology (see illustration on the following page). Rather than utilizing a single monolithic application or database, the Information Factory is assembled on demand from a montage of legacy applications and data sources that have been encapsulated as components.

Each CWC Strategic Partner will utilize the Information Factory Methodology in deploying their systems over a minimum period of two years. These systems have demanding requirements, but they adapt quickly to new usage profiles, require minimal staff training, and operate reliably in diverse environments. Each Strategic Partner domain presents a wide range of test and validation environments for driving successive generations of ComponentWare technology. Strategic Partners expect that ComponentWare will result in significant reductions in the cost of system testing and requirements validation for their demanding systems.

The key success criteria of the Information Factory Methodology is how well it supports new applications and changing user requirements and achieves reliability through the reuse of verified components. Data analysis and modeling systems are ideal domains in which to challenge these innovations. Application data is evolving beyond traditional numerical data to encompass a wide array of graphical,

---

ObjectPump is a registered trademark of I-Kinetics, Inc. ComponentWare and Ready-To-Run are trademarks of I-Kinetics, Inc. Orbix is a registered trademark of IONA Technologies, Ltd. ORBitize is a trademark of NetLinks Technology, Inc. All other trademarks are property of their respective owners.

audio, signal, and image data types. A key capability is the run-time (dynamic) generation of components for legacy data and applications. Another is the compile-time (static) generation of components for legacy codes and applications.

Each CWC Technology Provider and Solution Provider contributes and integrates key ComponentWare technologies. IONA, the current CORBA market leader, will extend their CORBA product, Orbix®, with high-

performance transaction management, object groups, and fault-tolerant services. NetLinks Technologies will build a new generation of ORBitize™, a comprehensive DOMS Interactive Development Environment. Heuristicrats Research will develop a range of security and data-analysis components. BBN Systems and Technologies, a division of Bolt Beranek and Newman, Inc., a leading Internet services provider, will be supplying collaborative planning components as well as high-speed internet

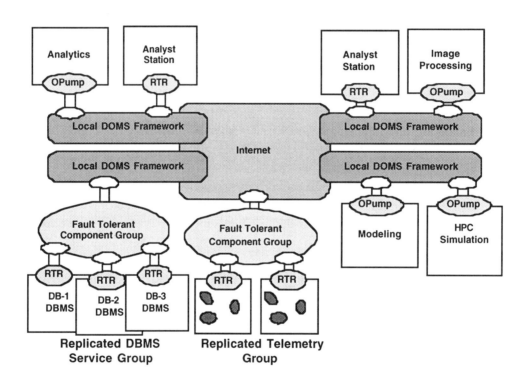

Figure 1. The Information Factory enables information systems to increase performance and functionality by dynamically integrating other application and data components. End-users (analysts) can access data and applications either locally or remotely through the Internet. The Information Factory runtime environment consists of specialized components, ObjectPump's Fault Tolerant Component Groups, and the Distributed Object Management System (DOMS) run-time environment. An ObjectPump (OPump) is a general-purpose adapter for creating components dynamically by encapsulation of legacy software code. Both Read-To-Run (RTR) Components and the ObjectPump act as mediators between the DOMS services and a native application module's specific control and data protocols. A Fault Tolerant Component Group is implemented by a group of replicated components. In this scenario, a fault tolerant database service is implemented using three Database Management System (DBMS) Components and a fault tolerant telemetry service is implemented using redundant telemetry feeds. Five different geographically distributed sites are shown, connected by both wide area and local area routers. Each site has its own local DOMS framework, applications, and services.

connectivity services. I-Kinetics will enhance DOMS integration tools such as the Object-Pump® and Automated Component Generator. The ObjectPump transforms a legacy application or data source into a component at run-time. The Automated Component Generator (ACG) is specifically targeted at existing software that has little or no DOMS capabilities. The ACG automates the generation of a complete component from existing code.

A key technology milestone for the CWC is "Ready-To-Run™" Components. CWC has already committed to Ready-To-Run Components for:

- *Data management:* Fame, Informix, ObjectStore, Oracle, and Sybase

- *Mechanical engineering analytics:* Finite Element Analysis, Computational Fluid Dynamics

- *Logistics:* CALS, regional maintenance

- *Desktop applications:* MS Excel, Lotus 1-2-3, Quatro, MS Access, AutoCAD, MS Word

- *Desktop developer environments:* Visual Basic, PowerBuilder

Subsequent releases of Ready-To-Run Components, ORBitize, and ObjectPump will incorporate the latest consortium member contributions in security, fault-tolerance, and workflow transaction management.

ObjectPump: Dynamic Synthesis of Object Interfaces

Member Responsibility:
I-Kinetics, Inc. (I-Kinetics)

The ObjectPump is a universal adapter for transforming data sources and applications into components for the CWC Information Factory

paradigm. The ObjectPump enables the Information Factory to dynamically synthesize new object interfaces at the time of configuration. Rather than utilizing a single monolithic application, the Information Factory is assembled on demand for the client from a distributed montage of applications and data sources that have been encapsulated as components.

The ObjectPump includes functionality for creating, manipulating, and transporting complex data between different objects written in different programming languages and running on different computer platforms. These services also supply automatic transformation and formatting of exchanged data. They are used as the basis for transforming from IDL data specifications, as well as standardizing exchange of data structures and their descriptions between the DOMS and local information system infrastructure.

ObjectPump Components integrate with other objects by exchanging both object-interface and data-format specifications at run-time. New interfaces resulting from the component integration can be created (synthesized) at run-time. The ObjectPump processes the required transformation between two different data interfaces. For the Information Factory, the ObjectPump acts as mediator between the target data source or application and the DOMS framework.

The ObjectPump's dynamic interface capability is based on a model of data-model independence. With data model independence, sometimes referred to as data transparency, an object can receive data from a foreign object without having to support the foreign object's data model.

There are two major methods for achieving data-model independence. Both of these methods require that the data-model specification (metadata) as well as the data be exchanged.

1. The data producer returns both the

metadata and the data. This requires the receiving object to transform the data into the required form.

2. The data specification is sent by the client object. The producer object transforms any returned data into the form specified.

Both of these methods will be supported by the ObjectPump Component's dynamic interface-specification capability.

Specific deliverables in this technical area for two releases of ObjectPump include:

- Functional specification

- Programmer guide and reference manual

- Application and deployment at Information Factory domain sites

- Binary licenses released to the CWC community

- On-going support, maintenance, and upgrades over the duration of CWC's existence

Schedule of Deliverables:
Month 6:   ObjectPump V2.0 (V1.0)
Month 9:   ObjectPump integrated with
                 Orbix+ISIS V1.0
Month 16: ObjectPump V3.0 (V2.0)

Orbitize™: DOMS Interactive Development Environment

Member Responsibility:
NetLinks Technology, Inc. (NetLinks)

NetLinks will develop and enhance ORBitize, a DOMS interactive development environment. ORBitize enables developers to create and browse CORBA IDL (object interface specifications) as well as to visualize object interface relationships. Currently, ORBitize includes IDL syntax-checking and supports multiple CORBA ORB vendors products such as IONA Orbix, IBM's SOMObjects Toolkit, DEC's ObjectBroker and Hewlett-Packard's HD-DOMS.

This task will result in a series of releases of ORBitize with the following functionality:

ORBitize Release 1.1

- Additional platform and CORBA ORB implementation support

ORBitize Release 2.0

- Generation and management of implementation descriptions

- Support for generation of language mappings for C and C++

- Support for Automated Component Generator (Task 3.3)

ORBitize Release 3.0

- Support for IDL generation from database schema and design files

- Support for Microsoft COM

- Support for generation of component test and profile instrumentation

- Support for object browsing and exercising

Specific deliverables in this technical area include:

- Programmer guide and reference manual of ORBitize releases

- Binary licenses released to the CWC community

- Ongoing support, maintenance, and upgrades over the duration of CWC's existence

Schedule of Deliverables:
Month 7:   ORBitize V1.1
Month 15: ORBitize V2.0
Month 23: ORBitize V3.0

Automated Component Generator

Member Responsibility: I-Kinetics

The Automated Component Generator (ACG) is specifically targeted at existing software that have few or no DOMS capabilities. The vision is to automate the generation of a complete component from existing code. Using a CASE-based methodology, developers will interactively generate COR-BA Interface Definition Language (IDL) specifications from the native data and control interface specifications of legacy code. This will enable developers to specify and create the data and control IDL specification of a software module. The Automated Component Generator will support the following areas of functionality for converting DOMS non-capable software into a DOMS-compliant component:

Control Specification: The developer interactively identifies which control functions are to be public (externally callable). The Automated Component Generator will have the capability of parsing the software code so that it can identify and present to the developer the candidate functions and variables for exposure in the public interface.

Metadata Specification: The developer captures the specification of the module data model and data types (metadata) and function parameter signatures.

Data Flow Specification: The developer interactively identifies the direction of flow of data (parameters, results, control parameters) into and out of the object. This specification step is required, as most development languages do not specify data flow direction because of the availability of a common shared memory. In a distributed system, data is moved from one object's memory space to another. A common shared memory cannot be assumed.

Object Adapter Generation: Once the three types of specification have been completed, the Automated Component Generator will generate a CORBA-compliant Object Adapter. The Object Adapter encapsulates the original software or data source, enabling it to become CORBA-capable. In some cases, a developer may be required to modify original code to disable (or enable) the original source code or binary.

For the scope of this work, the Automated Component Generator will support C and C++. The Automated Component Generator capability will be integrated into NetLink's ORBitize IDE tool (integrated development environment). Specific deliverables in this technical area include:

- Functional specification

- Programmer guide and reference manual

- Demonstration examples

- Binary licenses released to the CWC community

- On-going support, maintenance and upgrades over the duration of CWC's existence

Schedule of Deliverables:
Month 15: Automated Component Generator V1.0

Orbix+ISIS: Object Group Management Components

Member Responsibility:
IONA Technologies, Inc. (IONA)

IONA will add a range of object group services as a basic set of Object Group Management (OGM) Components. A small, well-designed set of such components can provide all the necessary support for different uses of object groups.

The building blocks of the OGM will be the IONA Orbix framework and the ISIS Distributed Toolkit (Orbix+ISIS). ISIS will supply a set of runtime services and a library of common protocols that coordinate client transactions with a group of replicated services. These protocols supply message ordering and mechanisms for maintaining redundant copies of shared state in a distributed system. Orbix will supply the CORBA compliant IDL compiler and runtime services.

The OGM components will augment CORBA with Common Object Services for concurrency control and transaction management. Multiple object $(1 - n)$ and group-based $(m - n)$ coordination and control models will be adopted from ISIS. The OGM component functions are presented in the style of existing CORBA functions.

Object Group Management Components will be used in load balancing, object replication, and other kinds of distributed coordination such as distributed management and control.

Deliverables in this technical area include:

- Functional specification
- Programmer guide and reference manual
- Programming examples and prototypes
- Binary licenses released to the CWC community
- Ongoing support, maintenance and upgrades over the duration of CWC's existence

Schedule of Deliverables:
Month 5:   Orbix+ISIS V1.0
Month 9:   ObjectPump integrated with
             Orbix+ISIS V1.0
Month 17: Orbix+ISIS V2.0

Fault Tolerant Components

Member Responsibility:
I-Kinetics

A set of components, collectively called the Fault Tolerant Components, will be developed. Fault Tolerant Component functionality will include the ability to implement a critical service as a collection of replicated components. Replicated services enable the system to continue in a gracefully degraded fashion if any one component fails. This task will be based on the technology developed in the ObjectPump (3.1) and Object Group Management (3.4) tasks.

Specific deliverables in this technical area include:

- Functional specification of the Fault Tolerant Components
- Programmer guide and reference manual
- Fault Tolerant Component prototypes for site domain Information Factory deployment
- Binary licenses released to the CWC community
- Ongoing support, maintenance and upgrades over the duration of CWC's existence

Schedule of Deliverables:
Month 18: Fault Tolerant Components V1.0

Security and Data Analysis Components

Member Responsibility:
Heuristicrats Research, Inc. (HRI)

HRI will develop a range of security and data analysis components. Specific security and data analysis requirements will be incorporated into Information Factory systems as required. Security site consulting will also be delivered.

Specific deliverables in this technical area include:

- Functional specification

- Programmer guide and reference manual

- Security and Data Analysis Components site domain Information Factory deployment

- Security consulting to the CWC community

- Binary licenses released to the CWC community

- On-going support, maintenance and upgrades over the duration of CWC's existence

Schedule of Deliverables:
Month 12: Security and Data Analysis
                 Components V1.0
Month 17: Security and Data Analysis
                 Components V2.0

Join Map–Server Component

Member Responsibility:
BBN Systems and Technologies, a division of Bolt Beranek and Newman Inc.

A port of the Joint Map Server to an existing DOMS framework is being done to create a base-level, sharable, common facility called the Baseline Map Server. The Joint Map Server is a geographic visualization tool currently being extended to utilize CORBA as the interoperability component. The extended tool is known as the Joint Map Server.

Functionally, the job of the map server is to render spatial (e.g., geographic) data and object-oriented, application-dependent data onto a display device. Currently, the map server supports this rendering function on X Window Systems windows and pixmaps. In addition, the map server supports queries on specific objects that have been rendered on the map to be made back to the original database. For example, in a map containing political boundaries, roads, and cities, a query could be made to the city database by the application, resulting in further information about that city being passed to the application.

The map server also supports real-time, synchronous collaboration among multiple users over a global network. Users see each others' actions in real time as they annotate the map with structured graphics (e.g., text, line drawings, symbology, etc.).

Other map server extensions currently planned or underway include the ability to view facilities data and engineering drawings such as .DXF format files within the same collaborative framework, and a port of the API to the Microsoft Windows environment, allowing client applications to run under MS Windows while the server runs under a UNIX/POSIX operating system.

The CWC effort will extend the Baseline Map Server Facility. This task is intended to provide assistance for practical re-use of the Baseline Map Server Facility as a CWC component, for inter-member transfer of technology, and as a real world DOMS and ComponentWare framework evaluation exercise. In particular, the map server extensions will be in support of performance evaluation and applications programming interface extensions to support the CWC framework.

This work will include noting potential advantages/disadvantages to the other Consortium implementations. Developing the Baseline Map Server will provide an early, concrete basis for evaluating the implementation interoperability of different DOMS, and appropriate development cost metrics will be shared with CWC members. This Baseline Map Server will also provide a contact point for technology transfer between CWC programs and technology.

Deliverables in this technical area include:

- Functional specification

- Programmer guide and reference manual

- Baseline Map-Server Component ported to a CORBA compliant framework

- Site domain Information Factory deployment

- Binary licenses released to the CWC community

- On-going support, maintenance and upgrades over the duration of CWC's existence

Schedule of Deliverables:

Month 6:   Joint Map-Server Components
              V1.0
Month 6–24:   Ongoing support and domain
              specific customization and en-
              hancements

Ready-to-Run™ Components

Member Responsibility: I-Kinetics, HRI, NetLinks, Pratt & Whitney

Domain-specific components will be developed for Strategic Partners over a two-year period. In addition, existing "Ready-To-Run" Components will be matured and deployed in the process of building Information Factories for NAVSEA and Pratt & Whitney and interoperability conference activities. The Ready-To-Run Components will incorporate CWC member contributions in security, fault-tolerance, and monitoring as they become available. Current Ready-To-Run Components planned include:

- Fame Component

- Informix RDBMS Component

- Oracle RDBMS Component

- Sybase RDBMS Component

- Excel Component

- Lotus 1-2-3 Component

- PowerBuilder Component

- Visual Basic Component

- Lotus Notes

- WWW server

- Internet Firewall

- BBN Map Server

Deliverables in this technical area include:

- Functional specification of each component in the form of written documentation and CORBA and OLE/COM IDL specifications

- Programmer guide and reference manual for each component

- Component binaries for site domain Information Factory deployment

- Binary licenses released to the CWC community

- On-going support, maintenance and upgrades over the period of CWC's existence

Schedule of Deliverables:
Month 6:   Ready-To-Run Components V1.0
Month 18: Ready-To-Run Components V2.0

Information Factory for CALS

Member Responsibility:
I-Kinetics, HRI, NetLinks

The Naval Sea Systems Command (NAVSEA), a U.S. government agency, will host the consortium's largest deployment project, a nationwide system for logistics planning and management workflow integration to develop, acquire, and support the U.S. fleet. System capabilities include: automatic cost estimation, funding and contractor schedule coordination, functional requirement and engineering design data comparison, product quality monitoring, and project lifecycle change management.

The CWC will be an active consultant at one or more NAVSEA site. Specific consulting tasks will include re-engineering consulting and deployment using CWC ComponentWare technology and open standards. The other major task will be the deployment of CWC technology elements at a NAVSEA site enabling the re-engineering of the site's information systems to provide a high-quality, enabling infrastructure that supports the organization at a reduced unit cost.

A CWC team will collaborate with NAVSEA personnel in the implementation of an "Information Factory" to integrate a wide range of NAVSEA's existing applications, which include project management, CAD/CAM, database management systems, spreadsheets, and word-processing applications.

Deliverables in this technical area include:

- Study of CORBA-based system life-cycle productivity

- Installation, training, and support of CWC technology

- Pilot CORBA-based Information Factory operational at a minimum of one NAVSEA selected site

Schedule of Deliverables:
Month 1–3:   Project requirements analysis, design, and planning
Month 4:   Testbed commissioned
Month 3–8:   Training, workshops, and pilot projects
Month 9–18:   Major project development
Month 24–30: Production rollout

Information Factory for Concurrent Engineering

Member Responsibility:
Pratt & Whitney, I-Kinetics and NetLinks

Pratt & Whitney will host an Information Factory for concurrent engineering. Rather than utilizing a single physical storage medium such as a database, the Information Factory assembles applications on demand from engineering product and process definition data components. An expected by-product of the Information Factory is a set of reusable components and data standards for engineering and manufacturing systems.

- Study of ComponentWare-based system life cycle productivity

- Installation, training, and support of CWC technology

- Pilot ComponentWare-based Information Factory operational at one Pratt & Whitney site

Schedule of Deliverables:

Month 1–3:   Project requirements analysis, design and planning

Month 4:   Testbed commissioned

Month 3–8:   Training, workshops and pilot projects

Month 9–18:   Major project development

Month 24–30:   Production rollout

Interoperability Workshop and Verification

Member Responsibility:
All CWC members

The CWC will host as well as participate in DOMS community interoperability activities such as workshops and conferences.
These activities include:

- ComponentWare interoperability test and verification conferences
- Joint Interoperability demonstrations
- Joint technology sharing
- Technical planning meetings

Schedule of Deliverables:

Month 6:   CWC technology sharing and ComponentWare interoperability workshop

Month 12:   CWC technology sharing and ComponentWare interoperability workshop

Month 18:   CWC technology sharing and ComponentWare interoperability workshop

Month 24:   CWC technology sharing and ComponentWare interoperability workshop

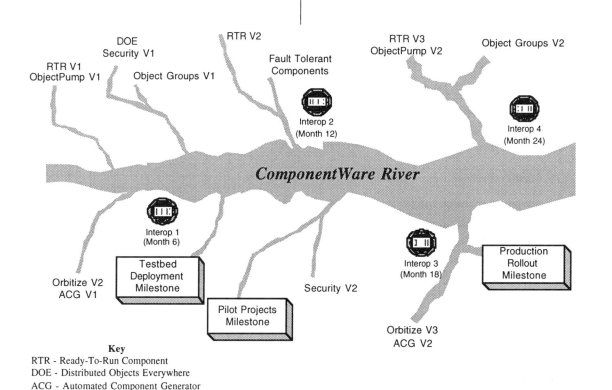

Key
RTR - Ready-To-Run Component
DOE - Distributed Objects Everywhere
ACG - Automated Component Generator

6 Months

Retrieving Software Components by Execution

Young Park and Ping Bai
ypark@cs.uwindsor.ca

Abstract

The building-blocks–based approach to software reuse typically involves the process of identifying and retrieving existing components that potentially solve a specified problem from the reusable component repository. In this paper we present an execution-based method of retrieving reusable code components in a large reuse library to provide support for more effective reuse in functional programming. The method is based on executing the function components on the input samples that are systematically generated based on program reasoning techniques, rather than as generated randomly or as provided by the user. The input samples are generated based on program reasoning techniques such as various inductions; one sample for the base case and two samples for the inductive step. The proposed retrieval is incorporated for reuse into a prototype software base system called *WiSeR,* which supports reuse-based construction of functional programs like Miranda programs and is available via the World Wide Web.

Introduction

Software reuse has increasingly been recognized as a promising approach to improving software quality and software development productivity [Bigge89, Krueg92, Tracz90, Mili94]. It is generally achieved by either the building-blocks or the generative approach. The building-blocks–based approach to reuse in software development typically involves the process of identifying and retrieving from the reusable component repository a set of existing components that exactly or potentially solve the specified problem. Many modern programming languages and paradigms provide a variety of features to provide support for building general and thus highly reusable software components. The functional programming paradigm uses, as basic building blocks, functions like those used in in mathematics, which thus makes it easier to reason about programs. It especially provides support for both using existing programs and building reusable programs through advanced abstraction mechanisms such as polymorphic functions, higher-order functions, and lazy evaluation [Bird92, Hughe89, Reade89]. As the number of reusable software components in a reuse library grows over time, the problem of effective and efficient retrieval of candidate components in order to facilitate systematic reuse becomes increasingly important.

There have been many approaches proposed to retrieving reusable components. Most existing component-retrieval approaches are based on using either syntactic or semantic descriptions of components. Syntax-based approaches to component retrieval [Henni94, Maare91, Priet87] are document-oriented and are based on keywords and facets. Semantics-based approaches to component retrieval can be divided into three groups; type-based retrieval [Park95, Rittr91, Rittr93, Runci91, Zarem95], execution-based retrieval [Hall93, Podgu93] and formal-specification–based retrieval [Cheng92, Luqi91, Mili92, Mili95, Rolli91, Steige92]. Cheng used first-order predicate logic as the specification language [Cheng92]. Rollins proposed searching through software libraries using formal specification in Lambda-Prolog [Rolli91]. Mili [Mili92, Mili92a] used relational specifications represented by logical formulas as the retrieve keys. Formal algebraic specifications have also been used as search keys for reusable components [Steige92, Luqi91, Zarem95]. Methods of searching for code components by using types of the components as keys have also been presented [Park95, Rittr91, Rittr93, Runci91, Zarem93]. Using types as search keys can be viewed as an approximation of using the full formal specification as a key.

In execution-based retrieval of components, which can also be seen as an approximation of full formal-specification–based retrieval, some sample executions of components are used as partial specification of the desired component and thus as search keys for finding components.

Podgurski [Podgu93] and Hall [Hall93] proposed methods for automated retrieval of reusable code components from software libraries based on actually executing components on a set of sample test inputs and comparing their output with the desired output specified by the user. In [Podgu93] the input samples are generated totally randomly from the argument domains of function components. In Hall's method, the input samples are provided solely by the user in any way desired [Hall93].

In this paper we present a method of identifying and retrieving existing reusable code components in a large software component repository to provide support for more effective reuse in functional programming. The method is based on executing the function components on the input samples that are systematically generated based on program reasoning techniques, rather than as generated randomly or as provided by the user.

We describe our approach to component retrieval by execution as well as a systematic method to generate sample inputs of function components. We also describe a prototype execution-based retrieval system that is incorporated in a prototype software base system for reuse-based construction of functional programs like Miranda programs and conclude with a discussion of some future work.

Component Retrieval by Execution

In a functional approach to programming, functions are the basic building blocks for building a program. As reuse-supporting features, most functional languages provide parametric polymorphic functions and higher-order functions. Parametric polymorphism can be seen as a mechanism for a greater abstraction over the types of the arguments of functions. The notion of higher-order functions can be viewed as a greater abstraction over the number of arguments of functions. Most functional languages adopt a strong and static typing system that has been regarded as important for building reliable software. Recursion plays a central role in defining functions. It is used to express repetition of computation instead of using iteration as in imperative programming. Recursive functions are generally defined by cases of two kinds; the base case(s) and the recursive cases where the results of the same problem with the simpler cases are combined in terms of applications of the function to the simpler cases.

Our model of retrieval by execution is shown in Figure 1. First, types are used as search keys to retrieve candidate components from a component repository (as in [Park95], [Rittr91], [Rittr93], [Runci91], and [Zarem95]). The types of argument and the results of a function component are viewed as a simple but incomplete specification of that function com-

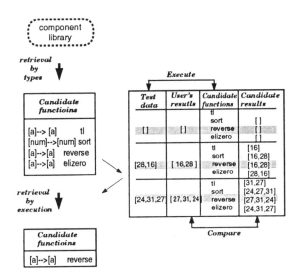

Figure 1. Component retrieval by execution.

ponent. In Figure 1, we need a function that takes a list of integer numbers and returns the same list of numbers, but in a reversed order, and we want to retrieve candidate functions from the component library. The type of our desired function is *[num]→[num]*, where *num* is the type of integer values and *[num]* means the type of list consisting of integers. Suppose that, using this type as a search key, we retrieve the following function components from the component library:

```
tl : : [a] -> [a]
sort : : [num] -> [num]
reverse : : [a] -> [a]
elizero : : [a] -> [a]
```

where *a* in the type *[a]→[a]* is a type variable, *tl* removes the first element of a nonempty list, *sort* sorts a finite list of integers into a non-decreasing order using quick sorting, *reverse* reverses a finite list, and *elizero* removes zeros in a non-empty list. Note that not only the functions of the same type as the query type *[num]→[num]* but also several polymorphic functions of type *[a]→[a]* are also retrieved. To further narrow down this list of function com-

ponents retrieved by types, we apply an execution-based retrieval in which sample executions of function components are used as search keys (as in [Hall93, Podgu93]).

Candidate components are retrieved by executing components on some sample inputs and comparing their outputs with the desired outputs, respectively. In this example, the components are executed on three input samples of the desired function's argument, such as

```
[ ]
[28, 16]
[24, 31, 27]
```

By comparing the outputs of the execution of each component in the reuse library on the sample inputs with the desired outputs provided by the user, i.e.,

```
[ ]
[16, 28]
[27,31,24]
```

respectively, the following function is retrieved as candidates:

```
reverse : : [a] -> [a]
```

Test data generation is a critical step in retrieval by execution. In the method of sampling behavior in Podgurski [Podgurski93], test data are generated completely randomly from the domain of argument. Random sampling mimics the operational input distribution assumed and may involve a large test input set, and it may take a long time to retrieve candidate components. Also, using random sampling may needlessly reduce the precision of retrieval in some cases.

In [Hall93], the sample inputs of the desired function component are provided solely by the reuser with the assumption that the reuser has good knowledge of the input-output behavior of the desired function component. Our approach uses the input samples that are *systematically* generated based on program reasoning techniques such as various inductions.

Generating Input Samples Based on Inductions

Proving that functional programs have certain properties—for example, proving whether or not functions satisfy their specifications—is often accomplished based on the reasoning principle of *induction:* (1) prove the base case(s) and (2) prove the induction step with the induction hypothesis. Various inductions are used in reasoning about functional programs:

- *Mathematical induction* on natural numbers for recursive functions defined over number datatypes

- *List induction* on lists, i.e., mathematical induction on the length of lists, for recursive functions defined over list datatypes

- *Structural induction* on recursively defined datatypes for recursive functions defined over recursively defined datatypes like trees

- *Fixed-point induction* on functions for higher-order recursive functions

In our method the input samples are systematically generated by mimicking these various inductions, i.e., one sample for the base case and two samples for the inductive step.

Samples for Data Types
Samples for the arguments of a function component are generated based on various inductions being used in reasoning about functional programs. The strategies depend on the type of the argument.

For the argument of type *num*, our sample generation is based on mathematical induction. Zero is quite often chosen to be the terminated case in a recursively defined function. So we generate zero as the base test case. For the inductive step case, we generate a value *n* greater than 0 selected randomly as the second test case, and the third test case is generated by adding one to the second test case, i.e., *n+1*. For instance, the example input samples generated for the argument of the desired function of type *num→num* are

```
0
4
5
```

For the argument of the type *boolean*, there are two values—True and False—so the test data is chosen either True or False. For the argument of type character, a character is chosen from the ASCII set as a test case.

Test data generation for the argument of type α *list* is based on list induction as follows. First, we generate the empty list, i.e., a list whose length is 0, as the base case test. For the inductive step case, we generate a list of length *n* greater than 0 selected randomly. The *n* elements are randomly generated based on the type of list elements α. We then generate a list of length *n+l* whose elements are randomly generated depending on the type of list elements α. For example, the input samples generated for the function component of type *[num]→num* would be

```
[ ]
[7,1,5]
[3,9,5,2]
```

Consider, for example, the input samples for a function of type *[[num]]→num*. The input samples can be generated as follows:

```
[ ]
[[3,0,7],[ ],[13,5]]
[[9],[7,1],[22,11,3],[22,3]]
```

The argument of type *tuple* (α,β) is structured by pairing two elements of type α and β. Test data generation is done by generating test data for each element and then pairing these sample values together through Cartesian product. For example, the samples for the argument of the type *(num,[num])* would be generated as follows:

```
0 [ ]
0 [11,5,7]
0 [9,5,7,2]
4 [ ]
4 [11,5,7]
4 [9,5,7,2]
5 [ ]
5 [11,5,7]
5 [9,5,7,2]
```

Test data generation for functions with more than one arguments can be treated in the same way as in the test data generation for the argument of type *tuple*. This can be done by generating test data for each argument first and then combining them together through Cartesian product. For example, the input samples generated for the function of the type *num→[num]→num* may be the product of the samples for *num* and the samples for *[num]*.

Similarly, the generation strategy can be based on the structural induction for the argument of any recursively defined datatype.

Samples for Polymorphic Functions

For the polymorphic function components, test data generation is done by first instantiating the type variables involved in the function's type with some specific types and then generating test cases for the instantiated type. Consider, for example, the retrieval of the polymorphic function of the type *[a]→[a]*, where *a* is a type variable that can be substituted with any type. For this query, we instantiate the type variable *a* with some type, usually simple, like *num*. The instantiated type query becomes *[num]→[num]*. The example test inputs generated for this query by the system would be

```
[ ]
[13,4,6]
[9,3,6,5]
```

Samples for Higher-Order Functions

Higher-order functions are the functions that take functions as arguments or return a function as the result. Test data generation for the functional argument is done as follows. We first do retrieval based on the type of the functional argument and use those functions retrieved by types as test data for the functional argument.

Suppose that, for instance, we want to retrieve a higher-order function whose type is *(a → bool) → [a] → [a]*. The type variable *a* is instantiated, for instance, with type *num* and the resulting type is *(num→ bool) - [num] → [num]*. The test cases for the first functional argument are generated by doing retrieval based on the function type *num → bool*. Suppose we have the following functions retrieved by that type from the reuse library:

```
odd : : num -> bool
even : : num -> bool
prime : : num -> bool
```

where *odd, even,* and *prime* take a number and return True if it is an even, odd, and prime number, respectively. Using these functions as the samples for the first functional argument, the final test data is formed by combining these functions and the test samples for the second argument of type *[num]* together as a two-argument function case. The final test data for two arguments would be

```
odd     [ ]
odd     [7,1,5]
odd     [3,9,5,2]
even    [ ]
even    [7,1,5]
even    [3,9,5,2]
prime   [ ]
prime   [7,1,5]
prime   [3,9,5,2]
```

A Prototype for Retrieval by Execution

The proposed execution-based component retrieval is implemented/incorporated into a prototype software base system for reuse called *WiSeR* (*W*indsor *S*oftwarebase for *Re*-use). The overall structure of the prototype for retrieval by execution is shown in Figure 2.

WiSeR is aimed to provide support for re-use-based construction of functional programs like Miranda programs. It is an interactive re-usable software base system that maintains an evolving structured repository of function components and provides features including retrieval, insertion and deletion of components, and the ability to browse the structured repository [Park95]. The user interface is designed to provide uniformity among windows

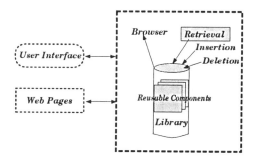

Figure 2. Overview of the system design.

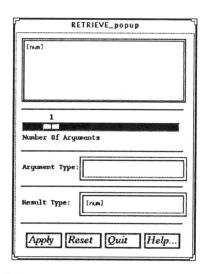

Figure 3. Component retrieval by types window.

and consequently attracts new, inexperienced reusers. All interactions are done through window-based and graphical user-friendly interfaces implemented in X-Windows and Motif. From the main menu, a reuser can invoke a number of useful dialogs such as the retrieval, insertion, deletion, and browser dialogs. It is also implemented with Web pages to be accessible via the World Wide Web.

Component Retrieval

To retrieve a function component, the user first provides the types of each argument and the result of the wanting function. Suppose that the user is looking for a function that takes a list of integers and returns the sorted list in an ascending order. The type query *[num]* $\rightarrow$ *[num]* is entered to the system through the component retrieval window shown in Figure 3. Then a list of candidate functions is produced by the system based on type-based searching. Figure 4 shows the candidate functions retrieved by type *[num]* $\rightarrow$ *[num]*. Note that not only the functions of the same type as the query type *[num]* $\rightarrow$ *[num]*, but also polymorphic functions of types *[a]* $\rightarrow$ *[num]* and *[a]* $\rightarrow$ *[a]* are retrieved.

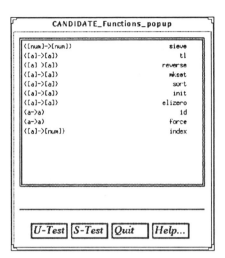

Figure 4. Candidates retrieved by types.

To narrow this candidate list by retrieval based on execution, the user has two options; *U-Test* for retrieval by execution based on the input samples provided by the user and *S-Test* for retrieval by execution based on the input samples generated by the system.

In using the system-test dialog as shown in Figure 5, the user is asked to enter the result value for each test case generated by the system. Figure 5 shows that the desired function should return the sorted list

[2,15,16,21]

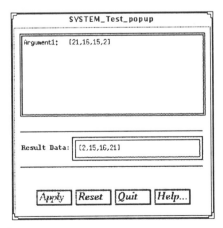

Figure 5. Compoent retrieval by execution window.

for the input list

[21,16,15,2]

generated by the system. Once the user provides the result value for the first test case that is shown in the list box and hits the *Return* key, the next test case comes up in the list box. The test data will be shown in the list box one by one each time the user hits the *Return* key. The number of test cases varies depending on the query and the type of arguments. After all required results are provided, the *Apply* button is released and execution-based searching will be started by clicking on it. By executing all components in the candidate list on the input samples and comparing them with the desired outputs, a refined list of the candidate functions is produced. In our example, the function called *sort* is retrieved as the refined candidates shown in Figure 6.

Component Insertion and Browser

When the user wants to store a new function component in the reuse library, the name of the function component, the types of the component, and the source of the component are entered. This process is done through the component insertion window in Figure 7. The button *Source Code* in the insertion window is

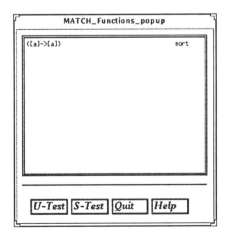

Figure 6. Candidates retrieved by execution.

clicked to insert the source codes. The source code of the function is then stored through the source window. Figure 7 shows the insertion process of the function called *exesqr*, which calculates the square of a given number.

A browser allows the user to browse the source codes of the components in the library based on the number of arguments. All functions with the number of arguments specified by the user are listed in the list box in the browser window shown in Figure 8. To view the source code of a function, the user just clicks on the function name, and the source code is displayed in the lower part of the

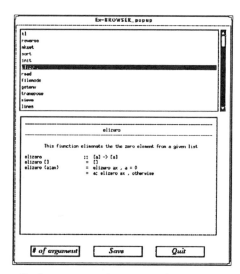

Figure 8. Component browser window.

browser window. Figure 8 shows the browsing of the function named *elizero*, which removes zeros in a given non-empty list.

Component Retrieval via the Web

Our execution-based component retrieval system is also implemented as Web pages with Common Gateway Interface scripts and an

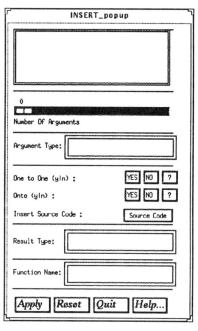

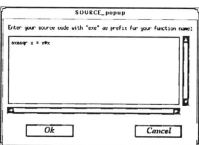

Figure 7. Component insertion window.

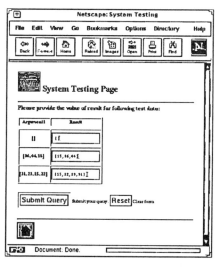

Figure 9. Retrieval by execution page.

HTML Fill-Out Form. Figure 9 shows the execution-based retrieval page.

Conclusion and Future Work

We have presented a method of retrieving the existing reusable code components in a large software component library to provide support for more effective reuse in functional programming. The method is based on executing the code components on the input samples that are systematically generated based on program reasoning techniques. The execution-based component retrieval proposed is implemented for reuse in a prototype software base system called *WiSeR*, which supports reuse-based construction of functional programs like Miranda programs.

We are currently investigating extending our approach to user-defined recursive data types and function components with side-effects.

Acknowledgments

This research was supported in part by the NSERC under grant OGP 0138415.

References

[Bigge89] Biggerstaff, T., Perlis, A., *Software Reusability: Vol. I. Concepts and Models and Vol. II. Applications and Experience*, ACM Press, 1989.

[Bird92] Bird, R., Walder, P, *Introduction to Functional Programming*, Prentice Hall, 1988.

[Cheng92] Cheng, B., Jeng, J., Formal methods applied to reuse, *Proceedings of the Fifth Annual Workshop on Sofhvare Reuse*, 1992.

[Hall93] Hall, R., Generalized behavior-based retrieval, *Proceedings of the International Conference on Software Engineering*, 1993, 271-280.

[Henni94] Henninger, S., Using iterative refinement to fmd reusable software, *IEEE Software*, 1994, 48-59.

[Hughe89] Hughes, J., Why functional programming matters, *The Computer Journal*, 1989, 32(2):98-107.

[Krueg92] Krueger, W., Software reuse, *ACM Computing Surveys*, 1992, 24(2):131-183.

[Luqi91] Luqi and McDowell, J., Software reuse in specification-based prototyping, *Proceedings of the 4th Annual Workshop on Software Reuse*, 1991.

[Maare91] Maarek, Y., Berry, D., Kaiser, G., An information retrieval approach for automatically constructing software libraries, *IEEE Transactions on Software Engineering*, 1991, 8(17):800-813.

[Mili92] Mili, A., Boudriga, N., Mittermeir, R., Semantic-based software retrieval to support rapid prototyping, *Structured Programming*, 1992, 13:109127.

[Mili92a] Mili, A., Mili, R., Mittermeir, R., A formal approach to software reuse: Design and implementation, *Proceedings of the Fifth Annual Workshop on Software Reuse*, 1992.

[Mili94] Mili, A., Mili, R., Mittermeir, R., Storing and retrieving software components: A refinement-based approach, *Proceedings of the International Conference on Software Engineering*, 1994, 91-102.

[Mili95] Mili, H., Mili, F., Mili, A., Reusing software: Issues and research directions, *IEEE Transactions on Software Engineering*, 1995, 21(6), 528-561.

[Park95] Park, Y., Ramjisingh, D., Software component base for reuse in functional program development, *Proceedings of the International Conference on Computing and Information*, 1995, 1022-1039.

[Podgu93] Podgurski, A., Pierce, L., Retrieving reusable software by sampling behavior, *ACM Transactions on Software Engineering and Methodology*, 1993, 2(3): 286-303.

[Priet87] Prieto-Diaz, R., Freeman, P., Classifying software for reusability, *Software*, 1987, 6-16.

[Reade89] Reade, C., *Elements of Functional Programming*, Addison-Wesley, 1989.

[Rittr91] Rittri, M., Using types as search keys in function libraries, *Journal of Functional Programming*, 1991, l(l):71-89.

[Rittr93] Rittri, M., *Retrieving library functions by unifying types moduloR linear isomorphism*,

Technical Report, Chalmers University of Technology and University of Goteborg, 1993.

[Rolli91] Rollins, E., Wing, J.,Specifications as search keys for software libraries, *Proceedings of the 8th International Conference on Logic Programming,* 1991.

[Runci91] Runciman, C., Toyn, I., Retrieving reusable software components by polymorphic type, *Journal of Functional Programming,* 1991, 1(2):191-211.

[Steig92] Steigerwald, R. A., Reusable component retrieval with formal specifications, *Proceedings of the Annual Workshop on Software Reuse,* 1992.

[Tracz90] Tracz, W., *Software Reuse: Emerging Technology,* IEEE Computer Society Press, 1990.

[Zarem93] Zaremski, A., Wing, J., *Signature matching: A key to reuse,* Technical Report, Carnegie Mellon University, CMU-CS-93-151, 1993.

[Zarem95] Zaremski, A., Wing, J., Specification matching of software components, *Proceedings of the ACM SIGSOFT Symposium on Foundation of Sojtware Engineering,* 1995.

Young Park is an Assistant Professor of Computer Science in the School of Computer Science at the University of Windsor. His research interests include functional languages and programming, semantics-based program analysis, programming methodology, and software reuse. Ping Bai is a software engineer at Hughes Aircraft of Canada. Her interests are software development and reuse.

Service Location in Multi-ORB Distributed Systems

Malgorzata Steinder and Krzysztof Zieliński
{gosia, kz}@ics.agh.edu.pl

Abstract

The main subject of this paper is service location and crossing referencing domains in a multi-ORB environment subdivided into technical and administrative domains. We propose an architecture that allows a client to find and establish a connection with a server in another domain. We present components of this architecture, their structure and functionality, and their cooperation with trading and naming services available in particular domains. The main focus is put on interoperability aspects: design and function of interORB cooperation modules and object reference mapping.

Introduction

The main subject of this paper is the problem of service location and crossing referencing domains in a system consisting of several technical (resulting from different implementations) or administrative (e.g., resulting from security) ORB domains. We believe that this problem will be critical with the forthcoming large applications that will be built over wide-area networks and will combine services provided by many vendors.

We present an architecture that joins trading and naming services of many different CORBA implementations and allows the establishment of a connection between a client and a server that belong to different administrative and technological domains. We address a problem of naming in a large distributed system, describe a concept of a federated name space [Yang96] and its application to a multi-domain system, and oppose it to the concept of global service names [Meyer96].

A Location Service resolves an object name to its reference. Object references are particular to the domain from which they derive. One cannot access services in other domains without a bridging mechanism that allows relaying operation invocations from one domain to the other. That is, services in multi-ORB system may be accessed only via a chain of bridges that are established when a reference delivered to a client crosses ORB boundaries. Bridges are also necessary at administrative domain boundaries, where they may function as security mechanisms.

The structure of the article is as follows. First, the problem of naming in a large environment is addressed. Then we describe components of multidomain Location Service architecture and address the strategies of name resolution and information that are used in this process. We also discuss object reference translation at domain borders.

Federated Names

Applications in CORBA-based systems are implemented by networked objects that are denoted by object references. The CORBA Object Model defines an object reference as an "object name that reliably denotes a particular object" and is used to invoke operations on objects.

This work was sponsored by the Polish Research Council under grant No. 8T11C01210.

To avoid the low-level concept of object references, CORBA-compliant software environments such as NEO provide naming services. Neither object references nor names specific to particular middleware are appropriate when crossing technological or administrative boundaries.

This problem can be solved by using federated names [Yang96] and a dedicated location service or by the introduction of a universal global name and interface reference space [Meyer96].

A federated name, apart from being the name of the object, contains additional information that allows one to distinguish objects with the same name that are located in different domains. In large multi-ORB systems, the concept of global names would be very difficult to apply. One may assume that object names are univocal only within the scope of a single, original ORB naming system, or within the scope of names assigned by the same user. On the broader scale, names have to be federated.

A federated name in a multi-ORB system should consist of two elements: a context and an object name. The context should contain information about the domain to which a named service belongs. There are many ways of building the context, but in our opinion, the context should reflect the structural organization of domains. In Figure 1, an example of a multi-ORB system consisting of NEO, Orbix, and ORBeline is subdivided into administrative domains by three users: dokis, dnons and moodb. The two presented context trees mirror different views of the system organization. In the first example, the most meaningful factors dividing the system are technological differences between domains. In the second case, the first thing that matters is to which user do services in a given domain belong. Other possibilities may also be envisaged.

Choosing a proper context structure must be thought through very carefully before other multi-ORB location service components can be designed, because this structure will have an impact on the organization of location service and on object reference translation.

A federated name does not have to be complete. Knowing that in a certain context a name is univocal, one need not specify more details; this allows one to search more than one domain or naming system.

The Location Service Architecture

Before a client is able to use a service located in some other domain, a reference of the implementation object of the given service has to be found and a connection with it established as a chain of interdomain bridges. When searching the system, the trading and naming services of

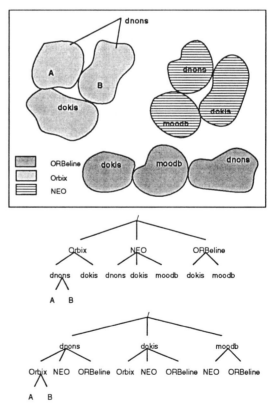

Figure 1. Federated Name Space context architecture.

particular ORBs are used. Of the three systems used in our implementation, only NEO is equipped with a naming service. In Orbix and ORBeline, either the trader or the name server has to be made available.

The architecture we propose consists of the following elements (see Fig. 2):

- *Domain Name Resolver (DNR):* Locates a required service in a given domain. It may be any name service or trader already existing in a given domain.

- *Federated Name Resolver:* A module responsible for forwarding a service query to other domains. This module may be invoked directly by a client or by a Domain Name Resolver.

- *Federated Name Resolution Protocol (FNRP):* A protocol of searching for a particular service in a multi-ORB environment that is used by Federated Name Resolvers to exchange queries.

Federated Name Resolvers constitute a federation that enables the searching of Domain Name Resolvers in many ORB domains. A Federated Name Resolver may be implemented for each domain or, if for any reason it is not, it may serve for several domains from which it is accessed via Access Servers, i.e., interface-specific bridges. All FNRs communicate using an ORB core built over IIOP protocol, which constitutes an ORB backbone.

Federated Name Resolvers are processes used for redistributing queries among domains, rather than for any real searching, which is performed by Domain Name Resolvers. A Domain Name Resolver is a specialization of a Trading Service or a generalization of a Naming Service that exists in a given domain. The Domain Name Resolver maintains a database containing mappings between federated names and some set of data describing an object denoted by a particular name. It is important to define this set of data. In our opinion it should contain:

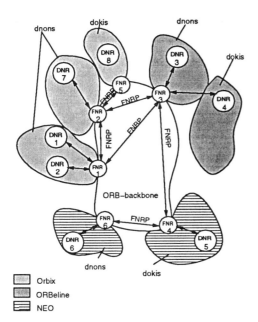

Figure 2. Federated Name Resolvers cooperation.

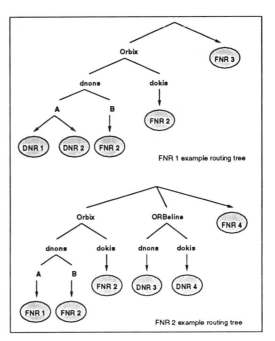

Figure 3. Federated Name Resolvers routing tree.

- A reference of the server object

- Interface Repository server data—information describing how the Interface Repository, which contains a definition of the object interface, may be contacted

- An Interface Repository identifier of the object interface definition

- Instructions for activating object implementation

- Object implementation access rights

The Domain Name Resolver obtains these data from a Trading or Naming Service, an object reference, configuration files, or a given ORB core. Once implemented as a server of ORB backbone, each DNR has a built-in bridge that allows it to cooperate with services of a particular domain. DNRs are in fact two-domain servers, invoked both by clients and FNRS.

A scenario of cooperation between all architecture components is as follows:

- A client contacts the Domain Name Resolver in its own domain or one in another domain via an Access Server.

- If the Domain Name Resolver finds a service, it returns its object reference to the client; if not, it contacts the Federated Name Resolver to which it is attached.

- According to the searching strategy, and assuming a name has been resolved, the Federated Name Resolver contacts one or several of its neighbors in the federation.

- A Federated Name Resolver that receives a request from another Federated Name Resolver contacts its attached Domain Name Resolvers to search the service implementation.

- After successful resolution, a target reference is passed to the client, being translated on each domain border that it crosses.

Translating object references is one of the most important problems when a system is built of more than one domain. When mapping references, not only it is necessary to find an understandable correspondent of the reference being mapped, but also a physical connection with the object in another domain has to be set up in order to allow requests to be translated and delivered to the server. Such a physical connection is established in the form of interORB bridges [OMB94B, Stein96]. Each interORB bridge possesses an interORB proxy object inside, which represents a server in the client domain [Stein96]. So, when a server is located by the trading federation, a chain of bridges has to be established from a client to the server before any operations are invoked. This chain of bridges follows a route by which a service has been found, but it is likely that this will not be the best possible connection between the two systems. Hence it is necessary to find and establish a connection that will better satisfy user requirements. To tackle this problem, two other elements have been added to the system.

- *Reference Translation Protocol (RTP):* A protocol that establishes a chain of half-bridges that provide reference translation between a client ORB domain and a server ORB domain

- *Reference Translation Server (RTS):* A server that implements the Reference Translation Protocol responsible for launching half-bridges.

In either case, a connection from client to server in the form of bridges may be established immediately—i.e., when a reference of the server is passed to the client (eager reference translation)—or may be postponed until the first need to use it appears (lazy reference translation) [Stein96, Hoffn96]. On each border between systems, a bridge translating operation invocations is set if such a bridge exists. If not, a connection is established via two half-bridges that communicate using ORB backbone.

Federated Name Resolution

Federated Name Resolution is a process of searching an object or a set of objects denoted by a federated name and returning its object reference along with possibly some additional data. The process is initialized by a client that invokes one of the Domain Name Resolver operations and specifies a federated name. The Domain Name Resolver searches its database; if no answer is found, a Federated Name Resolver is contacted. Federated Name Resolvers communicate with each other using IIOP protocol on the bottom of the backbone ORB.

Information about connections between Federated Name Resolvers is distributed among FNRs in the form of routing tables. The routing table of the FNR may be represented by what is called a routing tree, as shown in Figure 4. These trees describe the decomposition of a Federated Name Space and may be used to define a searching strategy. They are constructed with the following rules in mind:

- The Federated Name Space context resolved by the given FNR is represented by a complete path from a route of the space to a leaf that points to a DNR database

- The unresolved contexts are ended with pointers to FNRs, where the resolution process should be forwarded in the next step

Hence, the information used by the FNRP constitutes in fact a collection of pointers to FNRs and DNRs. For a small Federated Name Space, it is very easy to construct routing trees that will resolve any name in two steps. For a larger space, they may be constructed in strictly hierarchical fashion similar to that of the Internet DNS service.

Each Federated Name Resolver has to make a decision about how to search for an object reference. It may:

1. Search the Domain Resolution Servers it is attached to when a federated name context describes a domain to which it belongs

2. Forward a query to a Federated Name Resolver that corresponds to a given federated name context

3. Forward a query to more than one Federated Name Resolvers that correspond to a given federated name context if the federated name context does not describe a domain in a univocal fashion

In the third case, it is important to decide what searching strategy should be used. The neighboring resolvers may be searched sequentially in a certain order until the first answer that satisfies a query is found, or they may be searched sequentially until all answers are found and then one is chosen that best fulfills certain requirements. Although, it seems obvious that parallel searching would result in a better performance, it is often difficult to decide what number of Federated Name Resolvers should be searched, and how the best answer should be chosen.

Querying an FNR graph is handicapped by the possibility of cycles. In order to avoid going round in circles, precautions have to be taken to disallow the same FNR to be searched more than once in the same query. The problem may be solved with the use of distributed graph searching algorithms.

Crossing Referencing Domains

The number of domain crossings is important mainly for performance reasons. In the phase of federated name resolution, the number depends on how the federated name context information is built. The minimum number of domain crossings at this stage is *one* if either the client or server belongs to an IIOP-based ORB, and *two* when the client and server do not belong to an IIOP-based ORB. The gross number of domain crossings may be limited by building contexts that at the highest level contain information about technological domains. However, most of the time, the searching algorithm contributes to a number of hops.

A client–server connection requires a set of bridges to connect the domains. Technological-domain bridges mediate requests via ORB backbone; they are generic request-level bridges. Administrative-domain bridges, depending on the given ORB features, may be

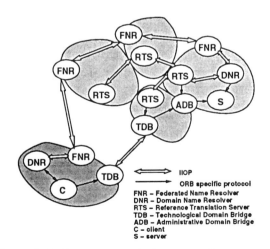

Figure 4. Reference translation scenario.

built at the lower level, and do not perform any sophisticated translations; therefore they are expected to be more efficient than technological-domain bridges. For this reason, when establishing a connection between a client and a server, first, the number of the first type of bridge has to be minimized.

The Reference Translation Protocol has to be organized in such a way that the number of technological-domain bridges between a client and server that belong to two different technological domains is exactly *two* (client-domain–IIOP-domain bridge and IIOP-domain–server-domain bridge) if both of these domains are not IIOP-based ORBS, and *one* if one of them is an IIOP-based ORB. Another reason for the existence of the Reference Translation Protocol is the necessity to limit the number of administrative-domain bridges so as to shorten the number of hops from a client to a server.

When a Domain Name Resolver finds a required server, it contacts a Reference Translation Server in its domain (see Figure 4). The Reference Translation Server contacts its partners in neighboring domains in order to determine the shortest transition to a client domain (if it is the same technological domain), or to an IIOP domain (i.e., to the administrative subdomain of the same technological domain that is able to launch a request-level bridge). Then a chain of administrative-domain bridges and a technological-domain bridge are launched, and an IIOP reference of a request-level bridge is passed on, as a result, by all Federated Name Resolvers that are used to locate a server until it is about to be delivered to the client. Then once again a Reference Translation Server is contacted to establish the shortest route from the client to the IIOP domain.

It is not always practical to establish a bridging connection between a client and a server immediately when a server reference is being returned to a client. Sometimes it might be better to postpone this action until the first operation on a server is invoked. This second option is called *lazy object reference mapping,* as opposed to *eager mapping.* Lazy mapping consists of creating valid object references that do not have support in any existing bridge. This is feasible in most of the systems we are familiar with; how it may be done strongly depends on a given ORB life cycle service. Lazy and eager mapping may be mixed together, allowing immediate creation of a certain part of a chain of bridges and postponing the creation of other parts till request invocation.

Conclusions

In this paper we have discussed problems that appear when many technological and administrative ORB domains are combined in a large system: naming services in a large multidomain system, locating services, crossing referencing domains, and establishing an efficient connection between a client and a server. We have proposed an architecture consisting of a Federated Name Resolver, Domain Name Resolvers, and Reference Translation Servers that allows integration and use of the naming and trading systems of many ORB implementations. We have also proposed a scenario of object reference translation combined with a topology service (Reference Translation Servers) that enables establishment of an efficient (and, for a client, almost transparent) connection to the server.

References

[CORBA93] CORBA 1.2 Revision Draft, 1993, *OMG Report 93-12-43,* Object Management Group.

[Beitz95] Beitz, A., Bearman, M., Vogel, A., Service Location in Open Distributed Environment, 1995, 2nd International Workshop on Services in Distributed and Network Environments.

[DOME93] *DOME User Guide,* 1993, Object-Oriented Technologies, Ltd.

[Harri94] Harrison, W., *The Importance of Using Object References as Identifiers of Objects— Comparison of CORBA Object References,* 1994, IBM Watson, TR.

[Hoffn96] Hoffner, Y., *Interoperability and Distributed Platform Design,* 1996, International Conference on Distributed Platforms.

[Meyer96] Meyer, B., Zlatintis, S., Popien, C., *Enabling Interworking between Heterogeneous Distributed Platforms,* 1996, International Conference on Distributed Platforms.

[OMB94A] ORB Interoperability. Joint SunSoft/ Iona Submission to the ORB 2.0 Task Force Initialization and Interoperability Request for Proposals, 1994, OMG Inc., TC Document 94-31.

[OMB94B] Universal Networked Objects, 1994, OMG Inc., TC Document 94-9-32.

[OMB94C] Interface Repository, 1994, OMG Inc., TC Document 94-11-7.

[OMB95A] ORB Initialization Specification, 1995, OMG Inc., TC Document 94-9-46.

[Orbix95] *Orbix Programmers Guide,* 1995, IONA Technologies Ltd.

[Stein96] Steinder, M., Uszok, A., Zieliński, K., *A Framework for InterORB Request Level Bridge Construction,* 1996, International Conference on Distributed Platforms.

[Uszok94] Uszok, A., Czajkowski, G., Zieliński, K., Interoperability Gateway Construction for Object Oriented Distributed Systems, 1994, *Proceedings of 6th Nordic Workshop on Programming Environment Research.*

[Yang96] Yang, Z., Vogel, A., *Achieving Interoperability between CORBA and DCE Applications Using Bridges,* 1996, International Conference on Distributed Platforms.

M. Steinder and K. Zieliński are with the Institute of Computer Science, University of Mining and Metallurgy, Al. Mickiewicza 30, Cracow, Poland. Telephone: +48 (12) 17 39 82. Fax: +48 (12) 33 89 07. email: {gosia, kz}@ics.agh.edu.pl

Black-Box Reuse within Frameworks Based on Visual Programming

**Bernhard Wagner, Ian Sluijmers,
Dominik Eichelberg, and Philipp Ackerman**

Abstract

Application frameworks allow structured reuse of object-oriented design and source code, provided that the developer understands the source code and has knowledge of the framework's design conventions. The notion *white-box reuse* refers to the process of developing software by writing subclasses with the knowledge and understanding of the internals of the parent classes. When applying black-box reuse however, new functionality is obtained by composing objects without knowing their internals, only their interface. We took the idea of object composition a step further by developing a visual programming environment for the easy reuse of a multimedia application framework's classes. Instantiations of these classes are represented as black-box components in our visual programming environment.

Introduction

The Multimedia Application Framework MET++

Our visual programming environment is based on the existing multimedia application framework MET++ [Acker95], which is an extension to the ET++ application framework [Weina92, Gamma92]. Event handling and message passing between the framework's objects fall under the responsibility of the framework and are already preimplemented. Within multimedia applications, events occur as discrete data resulting from user interaction, from data being read off storage media and from external input devices such as the mouse, keyboard, and MIDI instruments. Values generated by time functions controlling the temporal behavior of media are also considered as events. Most standard multimedia application functionality is provided, including time synchronization and multimedia-specific user interaction as well as multiple undo of commands and standard editor functions such as cut/copy/paste and drag&drop. A variety of editors is readily available for all supported media, so the media-specific manipulation can be reused by the application programmer.

Object Composition in Application Frameworks

Black-box reuse or reuse by instantiation is easier to apply than white-box reuse, since the internals of the involved classes don't have to be understood, only their interfaces. If several objects are linked in a black-box manner, the term *object composition* is often used. Through object composition it is possible to change a constellation of objects at runtime. Also, object composition is a valuable alternative to multiple inheritance when properties of several classes should be combined. In ET++ and MET++, object composition is heavily used. While black-box reuse is easier to apply than white-box reuse, the understanding of the interplay between instantiated black-box components is harder than understanding an inheritance hierarchy by looking at the source code of the involved classes. For this reason runtime-debugging support has been integrated into ET++, allowing display of the actual composition of objects in a running application [Gamma92].

Visual Object Composition

Our experience has shown that programming of applications based on application frameworks like MET++ is difficult to learn. The difficulty in teaching and encouraging blackbox reuse of MET++ classes leads to the idea of representing the reusable objects as graphical components with their interconnections depicted as wires. This method of presenting the possibilities and supported media of MET++ is much more playful and intuitive than confronting a newcomer with the bare C++ interfaces. The idea of object composition is presented in an interactive graphical way.

Wrappers

To make the existing framework's classes available in the visual programming environment, we applied the Wrapper or Adapter design pattern [Gamma95]. Wrappers are used to offer a different interface for an existing class. The Wrapper technology has successfully been applied before in MET++ for wrapping multimedia time-dependent data streams, e.g., audio, MIDI, video, time functions for the control of geometric aspects of 2-D and 3-D graphics. The new interface allows wrapped classes to be combined into a generic temporal layout system. Whenever a new time-dependent object is developed and properly wrapped (i.e., by implementing a set of abstract methods for start, stop, calculation of durations, etc.), it can be used in the existing temporal layout system without changing the latter [Acker95]. The visual programming environment also requires a specific interface, so the Wrapper design pattern was applied here as well. Now all media that have been prepared for usage in the visual programming environment have two kinds of wrappers: a temporal wrapper and a visual programming wrapper.

These two kinds of wrappers represent orthogonal access methods to the wrapped media. An application of this orthogonality is shown in Figure 1. The temporal wrapper shows an (interpolated) time function to control the z rotation of the small gear in the MET++ Time Composition View. The Visual Program below it shows two data units that wrap the two gears. The small gear is controlled by the time function and the changes are propagated through a scaling of -0.5 to adapt the rotation speed for the larger and slower gear. In a conventional animation system, the two gears would have to be animated separately, and if one gear's speed should change, the speed of the other would have to be adapted manually. In our environment the *relations* between objects are specified in the visual program and only the keyplayers are animated. The relations defined in the visual program are maintained, allowing one to specify animations redundancy-free. Animations can thus be specified and manipulated in a more structured way than animating each object with its own time function.

Building Blocks

A visual program in our environment is defined by a data flow diagram. The components of a visual program are *data units* receiving, generating, or processing events. New instances of data units that wrap objects of the framework can be created in a specific editor with menu and drag&drop commands. They appear as two-dimensional graphic representations and can be wired on the screen. Bi-directional connections are made between ports belonging to different data units to allow communication between them. Ports have a title prompting their meaning to the user and an arrow-like representation that determines whether they are meant for input, output, or both.

Object wrappers are grouped according to their purpose, i.e., *data repositories*, *filters*, and *mappers*.

- *Data repositories* include all kinds of discrete data including a number of file formats, arrays, single data elements, constants, user interface components, and system functions (e.g., timers) that generate events and hardware port access, e.g., reading input from MIDI and audio ports.

- *Filters* are a collection of data processing units. They perform functions on data either in the mathematical sense or as control structures with built-in conditions (for example, if-then-else and thresholds).

- *Mappers* provide capability to map data to different kinds of representations (e.g., 3-D graphics, 2-D bitmaps, text tables, audio, and MIDI output).

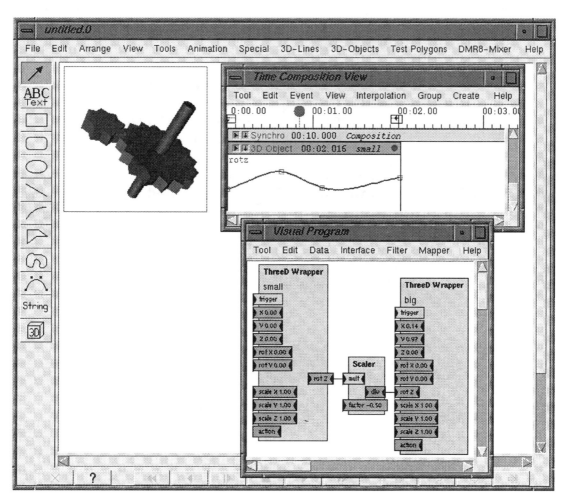

Figure 1. A temporal wrapper for a 3D object in the MET++ Time Composition View for animation and two wrappers for manipulation from within a Visual Program.

Executable Documents

Certain wrappers include user interface components that can be detached from the data unit's representation. They may even be separated completely from the visual program by dragging-and-dropping them into a dedicated user interface window. A button is provided to highlight the component if it needs to be located among others. These features provide the basis for a flexible user interface builder where executable documents can be created. Executable documents contain multimedia data types such as text, GUI elements, audio, animations, etc., whose behavior is controlled by visual programs. The appearance of GUI components is also visually programmed (e.g., the radio buttons on the left side of Figure 2 were defined by sending character strings to its "append" port). Text entries can be removed by sending a number as index to the "delete" port. Check boxes and pop-up menus are defined in the same way.

A simple typical example for an executable document is the Celsius to Fahrenheit converter shown in Figure 3. The dynamics of such executable documents rely on object composition only; no compiling, linking, or script interpretation is needed. As soon as the user creates a new instance of an object in the visual editor, it "comes to life" and reacts on any messages passed to it or any interaction via its user interface. In this sense, visual programming moves up to a higher level of abstraction as the future user of a program and its developer can communicate interactively while implementing and designing the software simultaneously. The specification and the implementation are no longer separated.

We consider these visually programmed executable documents as an alternative to Web-programming languages such as Java and CGI. While these languages still require programming skills, our environment allows one to visually specify a page's behavior. A Web-browser that supports this kind of executable documents as plug-ins has been developed.

Data Flow

The object-oriented principle (making the objects responsible for their functionality and for only passing messages) is transferred to the design of our visual programming environment.

This does lead to specific problems concerning the order of execution in a program. Triggering and data type conversion is strictly handled locally within the ports of the wrapper. Data types are kept simple. Only stan-

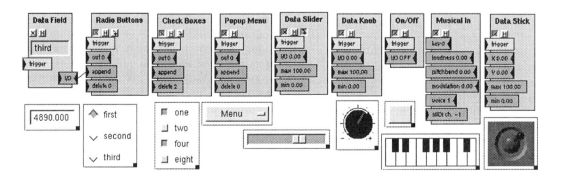

Figure 2. Examples of GUI components wrapped as data units.

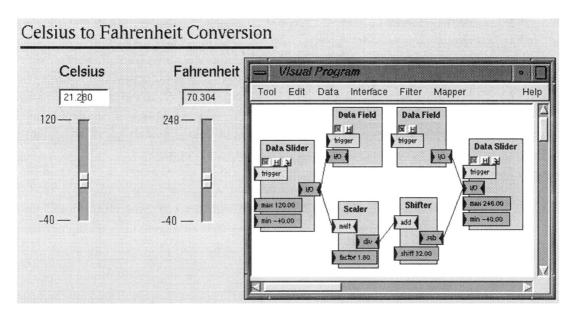

Figure 3. A visual program that implements Celsius to Fahrenheit conversion. GUI components of the data units are detached and placed into another window with drag&drop.

dard numeric and alphanumeric types are used. No sending of scripts or specific synchronization triggers is needed. A locking mechanism prevents messages from looping endlessly in cyclic connection patterns. This would occur due to back and forth triggering as events are passed bidirectionally.

Bidirectionality

Data-flow diagrams and similar representations usually contain *directed* connections, allowing the flow of data in one direction only. Our approach provides bidirectional connections between data units, allowing them to pass messages in both directions regardless of their position in the data flow. This implies bidirectional behavior of data units.

Data are units acting as data repositories (array, NetCDF file [NetCDF], database), event generators (timer, clock, music in/out, random, audio in/out), and user interface components (entry fields, sliders, knobs, joystick,

different kinds of buttons). Bidirectionality is possible for repositories: They can be read and written. User-interface components are bidirectional as well: If a certain value is fired at their I/O port, the corresponding state is depicted in the visual component. Event generators do not allow bidirectionality.

Filters need to be bidirectional, because they are placed in the path of data flow. Data can pass through them both ways. If the *Filter's* function has an inverse function defined, it will be performed if data arrives at the *output port* instead of the *input port*. A class has to be wrapped to make it compatible with the visual programming environment. Wrapping here mainly consists of implementing the abstract methods

```
EvaluateIndependentValues()
```

and

```
EvaluateDependentValues()
```

which are called when all dependent or independent ports have been set, respectively. In the case of a filter for calculating the *sin* function,

```
EvaluateDependentValues()
```

calculates the *sin(x)* function and

```
EvaluateIndependentValues()
```

calculates the *arcsin(y)* function using the provided independent value *x*, or dependent value *y*, respectively.

Mappers are designed to read data from a set of input ports and map it to a specific visualization or sonification. This interface generally provides an interactive mode, allowing the manipulation of the visual representations. The resulting events will be sent out of the ports of the mapper, invoking an update of any connected object.

Bidirectional behavior can be inhibited for special situations. For example, it may not be desirable to write to certain files or to change the system time.

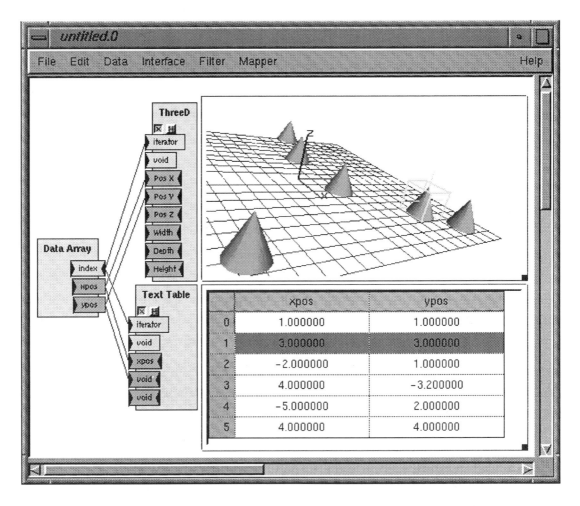

Figure 4. Bidirectional data flow between a data array, a 3-D view, and a spreadsheet.

The example in Figure 4 illustrates the bi-directional behavior of mappers, given an array containing five sets of 2-D data. It is represented by an independent port ranging from 0 to 4 and two dependent ports, one supplying x values, the second supplying y values. To map this array to a three-dimensional representation, the mapper's iterator port is connected to the index of the array, the dependent ports one by one to the x and y ports of the mapper. As a result, five 3-D objects would become visible each at their own coordinates in the 3-D space.

Each dependent port of a mapper has its default value in case nothing is connected to it. In Figure 4, the z-coordinate remains zero; width, depth, and height remain 1. The array is also connected to a text table mapper. The 3-D elements can be moved within the 3-D space to change values of the array. Such changes are immediately reflected in the table. At the same time, editing of values in the table will force updates of the 3-D view.

Triggering of Data Units

Some visual programming environments use specific control types, e.g., "BANG" in Max [Zicar95] and "PING" in HP VEE [Helse95]. This kind of explicit control information can be useful in developing real-time applications, but has the disadvantage that it has to be handled separately. It implies another step of thinking in developing programs, because the firing of data can result in bugs if a function is programmed to fire before it has received all the data it needs.

Our approach has neither specific control types nor is the order of execution dependent on the placement of the objects in the editor. It has a simple philosophy: everything is handled locally within the data units. Each port has a trigger that is either set or reset. A data unit will fire whenever all its independent ports or, in the other direction, when all its dependent ports have received data, meaning they have been triggered. The underlying object's firing method will call the firing method of the connected objects, whose firing method will do the same and so on until every object has fired. Since links are bidirectional, this could result in back-and-forth firing ad infinitum. To avoid this, a locking mechanism is implemented in the port. Infinite loops can be avoided this way and "wild" cyclic connection patterns cause no harmful effects.

Independent and Dependent Ports

In the editor of our visual programming environment, data units provide ports for their interconnection. Common data units use two types of ports: *independent* and *dependent*. The type is indicated by a defined color of the port's representation. For data units acting as data repositories *(data)* and representing the contents of files and arrays, a set of independent and dependent ports is generally used for addressing the data. The independent ports work like indices of an array (or record). The dependent ports behave like the array's values. A data unit evaluates its dependent values as soon as all its independent ports' triggers are set. Still considering the array example, this would mean that the value or the set of values at the indexed position in the array would be fired as soon as all its indices are set. To maintain bidirectionality, the firing can be induced by triggering the dependent ports with a set of values. As soon as they are all triggered, the corresponding independent indices are searched and fired from the independent ports.

Filters typically are functions; a great many of them are mathematical functions. For simplicity, only one-dimensional filters are described (and implemented so far):

```
y = f(x)
```

where x is the independent value, and y is dependent. The filters have one independent and one dependent port. Their triggering behavior is simple: when a value x arrives at the independent port, f(x) is fired from the dependent port. The opposite direction may be possible if the corresponding inverse filter function x = f -1(y) is defined and if f -1(y) is fired from the independent port.

Mathematically expressed, the relationship between independent and dependent ports can be represented as a set of n functions of arity m >= 1:

```
(y1, y2, ..., yn) = f(x1, x2, ...,
xm); (1)
```

where x_i are the independent and y_j the dependent variables and n is not necessarily equal to m. Each of the independent variables x_i has its own domain d_i with cardinality X_i and each of the dependent variables y_j has its range r_j with cardinality Y_j. In different terms, the set of ranges r_j can be regarded as a family indexed by the cartesian product (product set) d of the domains d_j:

```
f: d1 × d2 × ... × dm → r1 × r2 ×
... × rn; (2)
```

The cardinalities D and R of the domain product set d and the range product set r, respectively, are calculated as follows:

```
D = X1 * X2 * ... * Xm; (3a)
R = Y1 * Y2 * ... * Yn; (3b)
```

This leads us to a specialization of the independent port: the *iterator*. It extends the role of the independent port, allowing *data mappers* to be built.

Mapping and Iterators
Mapping is invoked as soon as a data unit is connected to a data mapper. For each independent port x_i of the data source, an iterator port is allocated in the data mapper. Each iterator analyzes the independent port it is connected to and registers its domain d_i. The cartesian product P of these domains is built, and D representation entities according to (3a,b) are prepared. Next, the elements of d (a set of index-

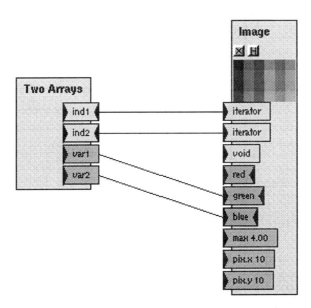

Figure 5: Mapping over two indices with different domains using an image mapper.

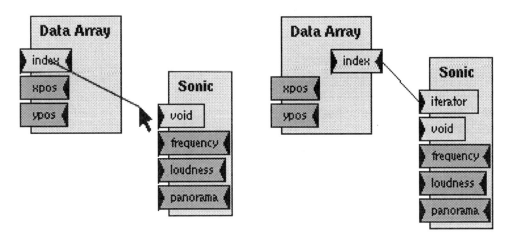

Figure 6: Connecting a mapper: dynamic generation of iterator ports.

sets) are stepped through and fired from the iterators to the data unit connected to the data mapper. The data unit responds by sending its dependent values corresponding to the received index set. The dependent values are then applied to the representations influencing their properties.

Another example will illustrate the mapping process (Figure 5): Two arrays, one containing six, the other containing four sets of values, are connected to an *image mapper.* Each array has one independent index port. The *image mapper* prepares D = 6 * 4 = 24 pixels in a bitmap representation and then iterates over all the index pairs making the data arrays fire the indexed values giving each pixel its color. Note that the source is not a two-dimensional 6 * 4 array, but two one-dimensional arrays of 6 and 4 values, respectively. The image mapper now combines each of the first array's values with each of the second array's values, resulting in D = 6 * 4 = 24 combinations.

A data mapper has a generic architecture to guarantee a high degree of flexibility when connecting data units. Different data sources can be connected to the same mapper and so the iterators and dependent ports need to be dynamically generated as connec-

tions are made. Data mappers have one dummy port marked *"void."* Connecting anything to a void port will make it change its name to "iterator" in the independent case or will take the name of the connected port if it is dependent. The void port is regenerated and stays free for further connections (see Figure 6).

Data Types

The data types *integer, short, long, double, float, boolean,* and *string* are supported. A data unit's ports hold meta-information on the data type used. Types are converted as the data flows through the program. If a port is not designed to convert to a certain data type (e.g., converting a string "anything" to an integer), a message box will appear on arrival of wrongly typed data, informing the user what type is expected.

The set of data types is kept simple on purpose. No message script types like in MAX [Zicar95] are implemented, because scripting components give the developer a certain "degree of freedom" that may let the complexity of the language get out of hand. The goal is to keep visual programming as visual as possible.

Applications

The visual programming environment provides several wrappers to existing classes of the MET++ multimedia application framework. It includes data units for visual objects, user- interface components, 3-D graphics objects, camera, lights, and time-dynamic media types such as animations and audio.

Summary and Outlook

By combining object-oriented framework technology with visual programming, we realized an environment that allows black-box reuse of an application framework's classes. This takes reuse a step further towards rapid application development. Visual programs can potentially pass messages to any object of the framework once a wrapper is provided for it. Acting as a general media patcher, the visual editor will enable events to be collected, processed and distributed among the objects of the framework. In the future, the visual programming environment should become a distribution tool of events in the framework, where anything can be processed and mapped to everything ("Media Patcher"). Visual programming can be used to define the behavior of temporal dependencies and user interactions and can also be used as a general visualization tool for data sets. Further work is going on to wrap more and more of MET++'s classes and to allow

the modularization of a dataflow diagram by creating sub-diagrams made up of diagrams themselves.

Visual programs in executable documents may even be an alternative to the scripting and program distribution that is now dominated by the hype about Java.

References

[Acker95] Ackermann, P., *Object-oriented synchronization of audio-visual data in a multimedia application framework*, Dissertation at University of Zurich, 1995.

[Gamma92] Gamma, E., *Objektorientierte Software-Entwicklung am Beispiel von ET++*, Springer Verlag; Berlin Heidelberg; 1992.

[Gamma95] Gamma, E., et al., *Design Patterns*, Addison-Wesley, Massachusetts, 1995.

[Helse95] Helsel, R., *Graphical programming: a tutorial for HP VEE*, Prentice Hall, 1995.

[NetCDF] is a special self-describing file format for exchange of scientific data across different platforms. It is maintained by unidata. See http://www.unidata.ucar.edu/packages/netcdf

[Weina92] Weinand, A., *Objektorientierte Architektur für graphische Benutzungsoberflächen*, Springer Verlag, Heidelberg, 1992.

[Zicar95] Zicarelli, D., Puckette, M., *Getting Started with MAX*, Opcode Systems Inc., Palo Alto, California, 1995.

University of Zurich, Dept. of Computer Science, MultiMedia Laboratory, Winterthurerstr. 190, CH-8057-Zürich, Switzerland, Voice +41-1-257-4569, Fax +41-1-363-00-35.

Automatic Load Distribution for CORBA Applications

Thomas Schnekenburger

Introduction

Typical CORBA [OMGJu95] applications are complex systems consisting of a large number of objects and using a large number of machines. Future systems will use more and more objects that are spread over more and more machines [Panca95]. Consequently, manual assignment of objects (either by initial assignment or by dynamic assignment using interactive tools) will be impractical. There will soon be a need for tools that provide an *automatic load distribution strategy* that can decide independently about actual assignments.

The general goal of load distribution is the assignment of *entities* to *targets* so that given performance requirements are met. Load distribution with respect to process assignment in distributed operating systems is a thoroughly investigated problem. See Turcotte and Kaplan [Turco93, Kapla94] for surveys. Furthermore, there is a large number of solutions for application-specific load distribution [Hamdi95, Hanxl91, Glaze93] and for realizing load distribution within runtime systems of distributed object oriented languages [Grims93, Becca90].

On the other hand, load distribution for CORBA environments is a new research topic. There are two important differences between load distribution in CORBA and traditional approaches in distributed operating systems or distributed object oriented languages. First, CORBA applications are "very heterogeneous," which means they may be composed of components with different programming models and different programming languages.

A single CORBA application may be spread over platforms with different hardware architectures and different operating systems. Second, the *implementation model* of objects is not explicitly defined by CORBA. Therefore, it is not obvious which parts of a system running a CORBA application represent entities or targets for load distribution. Nevertheless, the CORBA object model as well as the class of applications that are implemented using CORBA implies some general properties for load distribution. The aim of this paper is to point out these properties by classifying load distribution requirements and concepts for CORBA applications and by defining a general load distribution model.

The paper surveys the possible components of a system supporting load distribution and classifies the objectives for load distribution. These consist of the non-performance requirements limiting the set of possible assignments of entities to targets, and the performance goals of load distribution. Although CORBA does not define a particular implementation of objects, the paper introduces a general model for CORBA implementations and the resources used by these implementations. This model should cover almost all practical CORBA implementations.

Environment

Figure 1 illustrates possible components of a load distribution environment. The environment can be partitioned into two sides: On one side, there is the *real system* consisting of

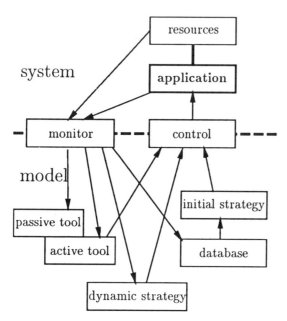

Figure 1. Environment structure.

the application and the resources that are used. On the other side, there are the tools for load distribution. These tools use a specific abstract *system model* that represents the real system.

Logically there are two components representing the interface between the real system and the system model. The *monitor* component collects information about the real system and transforms this information into the system model. Obviously, not the entire system, but only those components that have an influence on the strategy decisions have to be monitored. For example, if the goal of load distribution is to assign workload to instances of a replicated server, it may be sufficient to monitor the replicated server but not the clients. The *control* component is responsible for seeing that the real system realizes the directives of the load distribution tools.

The monitor information is used by different load-distribution tools. *Passive tools* just observe system behavior, whereas *active tools* are used by an administrator to dynamically control the system. The most important com-

ponent (see above) is the *dynamic strategy,* which independently decides about the actual assignment of new entities and the migration of existing entities to new targets. If a system is started, the initial assignment of components plays an important role because it is often impossible or at least expensive to dynamically migrate entities to other targets. Therefore, the environment may provide a *initial strategy* that uses database information about previous runs of the application to automatically find good initial assignments.

Note that this structure is only a logical description that does not reflect the realization. For example, the monitor component may be composed of a library that is bound to the application and a hardware monitor for the communication network.

Requirements

A load distribution strategy tries to assign *entities* to *targets* so that the system achieves "optimal" performance. Although the primary goal of load distribution is performance, there are four other classes of more important requirements limiting the set of possible assignments:

- **Functional restrictions:** Entities can generally not be assigned to any target.

- **Security:** Security requirements pose additional restrictions for possible assignments.

- **Fault tolerance:** Entities should be assigned so that a correct functional behavior of the application is guaranteed even if certain faults occur.

- **Real-time requirements:** Entities should be assigned so that the system can answer specific requests within a certain time interval.

The four points mentioned above can be regarded as a "priority list" for load distribution—that is, a load distribution strategy has to consider functional restrictions, security requirements, fault tolerance, and real-time requirements before the performance goal is considered. Therefore, load-distribution strategies can be classified according to their ability to take into account the requirements mentioned above. In the following, each of the requirements and its implications for the set of possible assignments is discussed more detailed.

Functional Restrictions

Functional restrictions are implied by the realization of individual components of the application and the ability to assign them to the components of the distributed system. Functional restrictions can be classified into the following aspects:

- **Heterogeneity:** In a heterogeneous system, some processes/threads can only be executed on specific machines. For example, processes may use a library that is only available for a specific machine type. Consequently, these processes have to be assigned to this machine type.

- **Local resources:** Resources (specific external devices, user interface, etc.) may be bound to particular machines.

- **Limited resources:** Resources (e.g., memory) may be limited so that only a limited number of entities can be assigned to a target.

- **Locality**: The implementation of entities may require that two entities have to be assigned to the same target (for example, due to local communication through shared memory).

- **Topology:** As a generalization of locality, the application may require that

entities have to be assigned to targets that are connected by specific links. For example, communication between two entities may depend on Ethernet instead of ATM, or vice versa.

All these requirements have to be considered for distribution—that is, the set of all possible distributions is limited by them.

Security

Security is the ability of a system to prevent unauthorized access or handling of information. In this context, important aspects of security are

- **Node security:** Security requirements may imply that critical entities have to be assigned to "secure" targets. For example, critical data should not be placed on a conventional user's workstation disk, because such data could be accessed by eluding the access rules of the application. This is similar to the *heterogeneity* requirements mentioned above.

- **Communication security:** Security requirements may imply that critical communication among entities has to use specific (or not any) links between targets. This is similar to the *topology* requirements mentioned above.

As with functional restrictions, security requirements limit the set of all possible distributions.

Fault Tolerance

Fault tolerance is the ability of the application not to show a failure even if failures of certain components arise [Kopet93]. To provide fault tolerance, the distribution of entities has to ensure (if possible) that the application does not fail, even if a certain fault scenario arises out of the set of all possible fault scenarios *(fault hypothesis).* A typical assignment restriction with respect to fault tolerance is that particular entities should not be assigned to the same target, in order to provide fault tolerance if that target falls.

Real-Time Requirements

In a real-time system, the duration between a stimulus from the environment and the response to the environment *(response time)* is time constrained. A real-time transaction (this includes all communication and processing steps between a stimulus and a response) must deliver the correct result at the intended point in time. Otherwise, the real-time system has *failed.* The main difference between real-time requirements and normal performance requirements is that real-time requirements are *worst-case* requirements, whereas normal performance requirements are *average-case* requirements. According to [Kopet93], real-time requirements can be classified as follows:

- **Hard**: Failures would be catastrophic. There are two subclasses:

  - **Fail-safe:** If a failure is detected, it is possible to stop the controlled system (e.g., railway signaling)

  - **Fail operational:** Even in the case of a failure, the system has to provide some minimal functions. (e.g., flight control)

- **Soft:** The consequences of a timing failure are of the same order of magnitude as the utility of the operational system. There are two specific requirements for soft real-time systems:

  - **Availability:** The system has to be available; correctness requirements are not very high (e.g., telephone switching)

  - **Integrity:** Even in the case of a system failure, integrity has to be provided (e.g., bank-OLTP)

There are two basic paradigms for accomplishing real-time requirements:

- **Guaranteed-response:** Given a fault- and load hypothesis, the system is guaranteed to work correctly. In other words, the probability that the system works without fail is the probability that the fault- and load hypothesis holds in practice.

- **Best-effort:** If a guaranteed-response system is economically not viable or if a reasonable fault and load hypothesis cannot be found, the system is designed according to the principle "best effort taken."

It is questionable whether hard real-time systems or guaranteed-response real-time systems will use a load-distribution strategy because these systems always consider the worst case. Consequently, systems combining real-time requirements and load distribution will be soft real-time systems that are implemented using a best-effort paradigm.

Performance

There are three typical performance requirements:

- **Response time:** The average response time (see above) of the system should be minimized.

- **Throughput:** The throughput (average number of jobs per time unit) should be maximized.

- **Resource requirements:** The average resource requirements of processing jobs should be minimized.

Unfortunately, the three requirements usually contradict each other. It is clear that reducing response time or increasing throughput will usually require more resources. But even response time and throughput contradict each other: To reduce response time, the processing of jobs (e.g., complex database queries) may be internally parallelized instead of being sequentially processed. In such a case, throughput is reduced due to the overhead for parallelization.

Entities and Targets

Many approaches to load distribution consider a very simple model of entities and targets: Targets are assumed to be *homogeneous* instances (for example nodes of a homogeneous distributed system)—that is, each entity can be assigned to any target. The job of the load-distribution system is just to assign entities (for example, processes) according to the actual load of the targets. A more general, but still very simple model consists of *classes* of entities and targets and *directives* specifying which entity class may be assigned to which target class. This model is used to represent heterogeneous systems.

CORBA, representing a standard for object interaction, presumes neither a specific programming model nor a specific implementation of objects. Consequently, a load-distribution concept for CORBA applications has to be general with respect to possible programming models and flexible with respect to possible object implementations. Our general model for CORBA applications is significantly more complex than traditional models, because it represents three system levels: CORBA objects, object implementations, and resources. Our model is a kind of classification, because concrete implementations of a load distribution system for CORBA will use a particular subset of it. The following section explains the three levels and describes some examples illustrating the model.

CORBA Objects

The CORBA programming model just consists of CORBA objects that are identified by *object references.* Using an object reference, an object may issue a request to another CORBA object. The CORBA standard specifies neither the implementation of objects nor the implementation of method activations. Even a *trader* is not specified—that is, rules describing how clients get object references are not within the scope of CORBA. Nevertheless, trading is an essential mechanism that will be provided by every ORB implementation. Therefore there are exactly two basic mechanisms which are relevant for load distribution on CORBA level:

- **Trading:** Given a "description" of a required object, a load-distribution strategy may select a particular object and return the object reference to the client. This corresponds to the normal definition of trading [Kovac94]. Trading may be integrated directly and transparently into the ORB.

- **Reference selection:** If several object references may be used for a request, a load-distribution strategy can select a particular object reference. The CORBA model defines that a request is always bound to a particular object reference. Therefore, the load-distribution strategy based on request selection may be realized either as an ORB-extension or within the client program.

Note that we do not consider the assignment of CORBA objects as a load-distribution mechanism, because CORBA doesn't have any definition of "assignment." Assignment will be important on the implementation level as described below.

Example

Consider a client-server system with a number of replicated and identical servers. Trading can be used for load distribution in the following way: Clients that want to issue a request to a server use the ORB to get a reference to a server object. The load-distribution strategy can now return the reference of the "least loaded" server. Subsequent requests of the client will now be addressed to this server.

Reference selection can be used for load distribution in a similar way: Clients that want to issue a request to a server use the ORB to get the set of references of possible servers. If the client issues a request, there are two possibilities, depending on where the load-distribution strategy is integrated: First, using an ORB extension, the client may pass the reference set to the ORB, and the ORB selects a reference and issues the request. Second, using a load-distribution strategy within the client program, the client itself may select an object reference and perform a normal request.

Object Implementation

The CORBA BOA specification defines several *activation policies* that describe some (but not all!) possible assignments of objects to *servers.* In the BOA, a server may handle exactly one object *(unshared server policy)* or multiple active objects may share the same server *(shared server policy).* Furthermore, each method activation of an object may be implemented by a separate server *(server-per-method policy),* implying that an object may be assigned to several servers. As mentioned above, the implementation of servers is not defined. Servers may be realized as operating system processes, but it is also possible to realize a single server by several replicated processes

or to realize multiple servers within one process. More generally, servers are realized by some *active entities* of the underlying operating system. As with the CORBA BOA specification, we will call these active entities of the underlying operating system *processes,* being aware that active entities are not necessarily operating-system processes.

With regard to the various possibilities for realizing servers by processes and for assigning objects to servers, the assignment relation among CORBA objects and processes may be specified as an n to m relation: a process can handle several CORBA objects, and a CORBA object may be handled simultaneously by several processes. With regard to object implementation, that means that a CORBA object is generally implemented by several *object instances.* Here we define an object instance as the representation of the corresponding CORBA object within a particular process.

Assuming that a CORBA object is implemented by a set of object instances, a CORBA request to that object will generally be transformed by the object implementation to a set of method activations to the object instances representing the CORBA object. This is the basic idea of the object group pattern [Maffe95]. On this level, load distribution can be realized by assigning method activations to the object instances (cf. [Banat95]).

Summing up, we have the following entities and targets for load distribution within the implementation level:

- **Processes** are active entities provided by the operating system representing execution engines for method invocations.

- **Object instances** (in the following text, just called objects) represent implementations of CORBA objects that exist within a process. Normally there will be a 1:1 relation among CORBA objects and object implementations, but it is also possible to implement a single CORBA object using several object instances and vice versa. An object instance is (by definition) assigned to (or "handled by") a single process (processes are targets).

- **Method activations:** CORBA requests are transformed by the object implementation to method activations of object instances (object instances are targets).

There are two levels for load distribution on the implementation level: Object instances are assigned to processes and method activations are assigned to object instances (and therefore indirectly to processes).

Example
Consider the client-server example mentioned above. The assignment of object instances to processes can be used for load distribution in the following way: All replicated servers are represented by a single CORBA object. If the client issues a CORBA request to this object, the object implementation generates a new object instance that handles the request. This is similar to the BOA *server-per-method* activation mode.

The assignment of method activations to object instances can be used similarly. The difference is that the object instances now are used in a manner similar to the BOA *shared-server* activation mode: A CORBA request is transformed (by the object implementation) to a method invocation of a particular object instance.

System Level
The system level of a CORBA application consists of resources which are used by the application and nodes, representing the distribution units of the system. The following para-

graphs discuss these components and the corresponding load distribution mechanisms.

Resources
The performance of an application is determined by *resources*—that is, there are resources (such as CPU, disks, or communication channels) that determine the run time of the application. Resources may be considered not only as physical resources, but also as a subsystem that receives requests and gives responses to the requests. Therefore, a resource may also be an entity like a particular process or a complete database system. In other words: Resources are just entities that receive method invocations (requests) by other objects.

For a given request, the implementation and the non-load-distribution requirements imply a particular subset of the resources that can handle the request. Consequently, we can form a *class* of resources by defining that two resources are within the same class, if requests to one resource can be handled also by the other resource. That is, a request is characterized by the resource class that can handle the request. For example, a resource class may consist of the CPUs in a system and another class may consist of the external storage devices. A resource may belong to more than one class.

Note that the fact that there are several resources that could handle a particular request does not mean that the request can be directly assigned to any of these resources. For example, a CPU request has usually to be handled by the local CPU. Assignment of the request to another CPU has to be realized by assigning the requesting method invocation to another node.

Nodes
The *distribution units* in our model are called nodes. That is, resources are either available for all method invocations within a node or they are not available for any method invoca-

tion. Of course, there may be *global* resources (such as a file server for several client machines) that are available for more than one node. Nodes represent also the targets for process assignments. This is the classical approach to load distribution.

Link Resources

Link resources model the communication infrastructure among nodes. A message that realizes a method invocation to an object on another node requires one or more link resources. Generally, link resources have a certain topology that reflects the topology of the underlying network. Messages between objects are *routed* through this network. The difference between link resources and normal resources is that a particular assignment can not only *assign* workload, but can also *reduce* workload by assigning communicating entities so that a particular link resource is not required. For example, two communicating objects may be assigned to the same workstation.

Implications of an Assignment

Using the definitions above, we can now discuss the implications of the load-distribution mechanisms mentioned above to the assignment of requests to resources. Processes, object instances, and method invocations are assigned (indirectly) by the strategy to certain nodes. These entities consume resources of a particular class. By selecting a node for an entity, the strategy can implicitly select a subset of resources of that class that may be requested by the entity. Remember that we always assume that functional restrictions are considered—that is, we assume that the assignment considers that there should be at least one available resource of the required class. Furthermore, the assignment of communicating entities to nodes implies the requirements of link resources for the communication between these nodes.

Replicated Resources

In some cases, there may be a choice within the resource class—that is, for a given request to a particular resource class, there is a choice which resource is used. For example, a node may be connected to a number of replicated, equivalent disks. Regarding link resources, there may be several possible paths for a message. In that case, the strategy may have the ability to directly select a resource.

Summary

The system level offers two possibilities for the integration of load-distribution mechanisms: The (traditional) assignment of processes to nodes and the assignment of resource requests to resources.

Examples

Considering the client-server example mentioned above, the assignment of processes to nodes can be used as follows: If a client issues a request, a new process is started (similar to the BOA server-per-method mode) at a lightly loaded node.

The assignment of resource requests to resources may also be applied to the example by modeling entire servers as resources. In that case, a server request by a client corresponds to a resource requirement of the client.

The Role of the Life Cycle Service

In the CORBA environment, the assignment of entities to targets is mainly treated by the CORBA Life Cycle Services specification [OMGMa95]. Therefore, this section discusses the role of the Life Cycle Service with respect to our general model.

The Life Cycle Service describes standard services for (remotely) creating, deleting, copying, and moving objects.

On the CORBAservices level, the targets for object assignment are called *factories*. A factory is just a normal CORBA object that is responsible for generating another object. Factories do not have standard interfaces. Object creation is realized by calling a particular *create*-operation of the factory. Clients obtain references to factories in the same fashion that they find any object.

Parameters specifying targets for moving or copying objects are not single factories, but axe so called *factory finders.* A factory finder is an object that represents a particular set of factories. Therefore, a factory finder might represent any set of targets for an object assignment, such as a set of nodes or a set of processes. To copy or move an object, a client calls the *copy* operation (or the *move* operation) that has to be implemented by any object handled by the Life Cycle Service. This operation may call the specified factory finder that returns a list of possible factories for handling the copy or move operation. The criteria for selecting a particular factory is not defined by the Life Cycle Service Specification.

Creating, copying, or moving a CORBA object implies that the corresponding object instances are created within, copied to, or moved to a particular process. Therefore, the Life Cycle Service Specification can be arranged into the implementation level of our general model. The factory and factory-finder model represents one possible base for realizing automatic load distribution on the object implementation level.

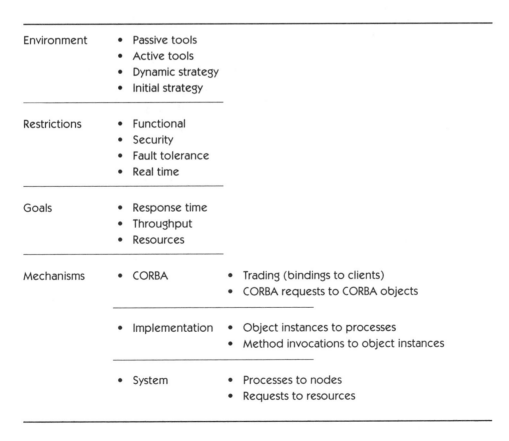

Environment	• Passive tools • Active tools • Dynamic strategy • Initial strategy	
Restrictions	• Functional • Security • Fault tolerance • Real time	
Goals	• Response time • Throughput • Resources	
Mechanisms	• CORBA	• Trading (bindings to clients) • CORBA requests to CORBA objects
	• Implementation	• Object instances to processes • Method invocations to object instances
	• System	• Processes to nodes • Requests to resources

Figure 2. Classification.

Summary

Figure 2 integrates the classifications in the previous sections. There are passive and active tools for manual assignment as well as automatic tools for dynamic assignment and for initial assignment.

Practical load-distribution strategies for CORBA at least have to consider functional requirements, since CORBA applications will usually be realized in heterogeneous environments. In many cases, security, fault tolerance, and real-time requirements have to be considered by the strategy. That is, the strategy has to provide possibilities for restricting the set of possible assignments according to these non-performance requirements.

The goals of load distribution may be response time, throughput, or resource usage. Although these goals usually contradict each other, they may be combined using a particular rating.

Load-distribution mechanisms can be classified into three levels. First, there is the CORBA object level consisting of object references that are delivered to clients ("trading") and CORBA requests that are invoked on CORBA objects. Second, there is the implementation level consisting of object instances that are assigned to processes and method invocations that are invoked on object instances. Third, there is the system level consisting of processes that are assigned to nodes and resource requests that are assigned to resources. A particular load-distribution strategy may use just a subset of these mechanisms.

Summing up, the different components, requirements, goals, and mechanisms imply an immense number of possibilities for systems supporting load distribution. The classification in this paper should help one to classify emerging load-distribution systems supporting CORBA applications as well as application-specific solutions for load distribution in CORBA.

References

[Banat95] Banatre, M., Belhamissi, Y., and Issarny, V., Adaptive Placement of Method Executions within a Customizable Distributed Object-Based Runtime System, *Proceedings of the 15th International Conference on Distributed Computing Systems,* Vancouver, Canada, pages 279-286,1995.

[Becca90] Beccard, R., and Ameling, W., From Object-Oriented Programming to Automatic Load Distribution, In *CONPAR 90,* pages 502-512, Zürich, September 1990.

[Glaze93] Glazer, D.W., and Tropper, C., On Process Migration and Load Balancing in Time Warp, *IEEE Transactions on Parallel and Distributed Systems,* 4(3):318-327, 1993.

[Grims93] Grimshaw, A. S., Easy-to-Use Object-Oriented Parallel Processing with Mentat, *Computer,* 26(5):39-51, 1993.

[Hamdi95] Hamdi M., and Chi-Kin Lee, Dynamic Load Balancing of Data Parallel Applications on a Distributed Network, *International Conference on Supercomputing,* Barcelona, Spain, 1995.

[Hanxl91] Hanxleden, R. V., and Ridgway Scott, L., Load Balancing on Message Passing Architectures, *Journal of Parallel and Distributed Computing,* 13:312-324,1991.

[Kapla94] Kaplan, J. A., and Nelson, M. L., *A Comparison of Queueing, Cluster and Distributed Computing Systems,* Technical Report Technical Memorandum 109025 (Revision 1), NASA Langley Research Center, Hampton, Virginia, 1994.

[Kopet93] Kopetz, H., and Verissimo, P., Real Time and Dependability Concepts, In Sape J. Mullender, editor, *Distributed Systems,* pages 411-446, ACM Press, New York, 1993.

[Kovac94]Kovacs, E., and Wirag, S., Trading and Distributed Application Management: An Integrated Approach, *Proceedings of the Fifth IFIP/ IEEE International Workshop on Distributed Systems: Operations & Management,* Toulouse, France, 1994.

[Maffe95] Maffeis, S., Adding Group Communication and Fault-Tolerance to CORBA, *Proceedings of the 1995 USENIX Conference on Object-Oriented Technologies,* Monterey, CA, USA, 1995.

[OMGJu95] OMG (Object Management Group), *The Common Object Request Broker: Architecture and Specification, Revision 2.0,* Technical Report, July 1995.

[OMGMa95] OMG (Object Management Group), CORBAservices: Common Object Services Specification, *Technical Report 953-31,* March 1995.

[Panca95] Pancake, C. M., The Promise and the Cost of Object Technology. A Five-Year Forecast, *Communications of the ACM,* pages 33-49, October 1995.

[Turco93] Turcotte, L., A Survey of Software Environments for Exploiting Networked Computing Resources, *Technical Report MSUEIRS-93-2,* NSF Engineering Research Center for Computational Field Simulation, Mississippi State University, Starkville, 1993.

Thomas Schnekenburger is with the Technische Universitit München, Institut für Informatik, Orleansstr. 34, D-81667 Müchen.

Mobile Agents—Mobile Components

Hermann Ilmberger, Jürgen Schmitz, and Sabine Thürmel
{Hermann.Ilmberger, Juergen.Schmitz, Sabine.Thuermel}@zfe.siemens.de

Abstract

Mobile agents are software components that autonomously fulfill tasks in a distributed system by moving between several computers, taking with them their program code and accumulated execution state. The basic motivation for mobility is to bring the data processing program as near as possible to the data to be processed. It may be more efficient to move a small or medium grain agent to a server where the data is located than to transfer back and forth many requests to the data over a possibly slow network. Complex problems can be solved more flexibly by combining different environments using mobility. A new field of applications is enabled in the mobile computing area. People on the move can be active in the net without steady online connection; mobile agents represent their user in the net. This paper elaborates on the relation of mobile agents to components, gives an overview of existing mobile agent systems and application scenarios, and describes the swarm intelligence technology: cooperating mobile agents for adaptive problem solutions.

Introduction

The inherent power of the world of networked computers is currently partially exploited by utilizing the well-known client-server paradigm. Independent software programs that offer a particular service serve requests from remote clients. This paradigm has now been shifted into the world of object technology.

The Object Management Group (OMG) has introduced a platform layer that enables the transparent access of (object) services across the network. Their Common Object Request Broker Architecture (CORBA) trades services by offering object interfaces and by performing the necessary call mechanisms, thus hiding (static) service location and interface details and forming a distributed object space. To build integrated network applications, the derived componentware approach is aiming to deliver the glue for composing distributed applications out of coarser grained objects, the components. The OpenDoc Glossary defines a component as "A self-contained, reusable software module holding both code and data."

Components with the ability to move are prepared for even better adaptation to the dynamic nature of network contents and services (Internet!). They wander through the network to fulfill their task, register at brokers, and announce their departure. They are able to perform more complex tasks by cooperation with other components and by spawning copies of themselves to parallelize actions.

Mobile agents are mobile software components that autonomously fulfill tasks in a distributed system by moving between several computers, taking with them their program code and accumulated execution state. Within recent years, quite a number of mobile agent systems became available. The meaning of the term mobile in these systems varies widely and includes various flavors, as we will discuss later.

The CORBA scenario (with extensions for mobile agents) is ideally suited as a (broker) platform for agent software, if we see an agent as an object. Smart agents are roaming around, visiting CORBA platforms and using services offered by different agents and local components, thereby exploiting the knowledge and facilities of (part of) the network. This finally results in shared problem solving, done in parallel and cooperatively, and implicitly programmed in tens or hundreds of agents.

This paper elaborates on the following issues with regard to mobile agents:

- Comparison of agents and components
- Flavors of mobility
- Agent mobility—how, when, why
- Overview of existing mobile agent systems
- Our work in cooperative multiagent systems: swarm intelligence

Agents and Components/ Distributed Objects

The term *agent* is used in even more contexts than the term *object*. The meanings of *agent* vary widely ([Frank96]), ranging from simple mail filters to intelligent control software for flight surveillance. Even if the diffuse usage of the term *intelligent agent* puts it in the same line with the buzzwords *multimedia* and *cyberspace*, there are some common and distinguishing features. The forum of the agent research community, the Software Agents Mailing List [SAML], also does not provide an authoritative definition, but provides a list of attributes often found in agents:

- *Autonomous:* An agent is able to take initiative and exercise a nontrivial degree of control over its own actions.

- *Goal-oriented:* An agent accepts high-level requests indicating what a human user wants and is responsible for deciding how and where to satisfy the request.

- *Collaborative:* An agent does not blindly obey commands, but has the ability to modify requests, ask clarification questions, or even refuse to satisfy certain requests.

- *Flexible:* The agent's actions are not scripted; it is able to dynamically choose which actions to invoke, and in what sequence, in response to the state of its external environment.

- *Self-starting:* Unlike standard programs that are directly invoked by the user, an agent can sense changes to its environment and decide when to act.

- *Temporal continuity:* Agents are continuously running processes, not "one-shot" computations that map a single input to a single output, and then terminate. This persistence allows them to gather experience.

- *Character:* An agent has a well-defined, believable personality and emotional state.

- *Communicative, cooperative:* The agent is able to engage in complex communication with other agents, including people, in order to obtain information or enlist their help in accomplishing its goals.

- *Adaptive:* The agent automatically customizes itself to the preferences of its user based on previous experience. The agent also automatically adapts to changes in its environment.

- *Mobile:* An agent is able to transport itself from one machine to another and across different system architectures and platforms.

In summary, a mobile agent is a piece of mobile software that autonomously and adaptively is in charge of fulfilling requests. The fulfillment is done flexibly, in terms of where the task is performed, how it is done, and with how many agents it is done. To distinguish itself from a computer virus, an agent has to prove its identity, which consists of interpreted code, and it has no access to critical system resources.

In our work we focus on autonomous, adaptive, cooperative and mobile agents, forming a swarm of entities. Their overall systems behavior is not explicitly programmed. It results from the behavior and the interaction of agents.

In the rest of the section we want to examine mutualities and differences between our mobile agents and the component paradigm, seeing components as coarse-grained objects that deliver a particular service by internal data and methods.

Mutualities

- Both agents and components form a distributed software system by means of entities spread over a network.

- Relations between entities are mediated—objects are mediated by an object request broker; agents are mediated by an agent platform (runtime environment for mobile agents for execution, communication, information, etc.).

- Both have a fixed interface.

- Both are self-contained: both contain their code and data.

Differences/Extensions

- Agents are able to be pro-active; they don't have to wait to be "triggered" by a method call like re-active objects.

- Agents are active entities, acting autonomously on behalf of a user or another program; they are represented by a process or a thread. Objects are predominantly passive entities, offering a procedural interface to other objects.

- Agents cooperate deliberately with other agents, exchanging knowledge and acting as client or server for requests. Objects cooperate deterministically with other objects, acting as client or server for method calls.

- Agents possess built-in "breed" functionality to generate new agents. Objects have no built-in breeding unless this is specifically programmed.

- Agents are monitored and controlled by platforms. There is no monitoring instance for objects unless this is specifically programmed.

- Mobile agents have the potential to roam around in a network. Objects are bound to an address and place.

Agent behavior is situation- and environment-dependent; they may act/react upon states/signals/messages autonomously according to their internal state and external environment; message protocols also facilitate reuse and dynamic linking of programs. Objects have interfaces to be called in an RPC-style; their behavior is deterministic and predetermined by the interface description.

Mobility

Mobility is a technical property of agents that can be examined separately from the other properties we have discussed.

Flavors of Mobility

When it comes to the definition of the term *mobile agent,* we see a broad spectrum in the literature.

In some systems the agent actually is a static software component sitting in and never leaving a mobile device. An example is a traffic guidance agent in a car or in a PIC (Personal Intelligent Communicator).

A second kind of mobility became popular with the advent of Java: a piece of software is pulled over a network from a server to a client machine. The program starts and executes at the client to fulfill some useful task. (This is in contrast to the UNIX remote shell command, where shell scripts are sent—pushed—from the client's machine to another machine in order to execute there in the local environment.) When talking about components, this model means that a requested component comes to the requester. All method calls are then performed locally. The Java language and interpreter when employed for applet programming within HTML pages implements this flavor of mobility, where applets can be fetched from the whole World Wide Web.

The Mobile Service Agent layer of the Facile system [Thoms95, Knabe95] extends this notion of mobility: besides allowing one to fetch agent code from a server to a client, it also allows the agent to keep a representative of itself on the server. By this means, the agent is able to act even if its client part is currently not reachable. An application area for this system is CSCW (computer supported cooperative work) in a mobile computing environment.

Knabe [Knabe95] defines mobile agents as "code-containing objects that may be transmitted between communicating participants in a distributed system." This flavor of mobile agents is a passive one. The piece of software is moved by a higher-level instance; it does not move itself by its own will or action.

The notion of agent we focus on in this paper is a more autonomous one. We describe mobile agents that are able to move themselves from one environment to another environment by their own action, without having to be triggered from outside, but of course using system facilities for transport. The agents can move at the beginning of their execution or during execution. Even multiple mobility for visiting a whole chain of environments is possible. While moving, they take with them their complete accumulated program state. Thus they can make use of this state in the visited environment or machine. Mobility in this sense can be interpreted as extending the agent's environment [Auer95]. All the environments/ machines the agent has the potential to visit are part of its total environment. Adding this kind of mobility to components means one can create active components that have the ability to go where they can perform their task best.

A number of systems that support this notion of mobility are currently available. We will describe some of them later in this paper.

Why and When Mobility

Within the last year a number of mobile agent systems became available. What is the driving force behind these developments? And what are their application areas?

The basic idea in these mobile agent systems is to realize and enhance client-server computing capabilities by moving active programs — not only passive requests — between clients and servers. New types of applications in the areas of mobile computing (users who are on the move), information retrieval, network management, distributed problem solving and electronic commerce motivate the use of mobile agents. An assessment of possible application areas has been done by Harrison and White [Harri95, White95].

Mobile computers—e.g., Personal Digital Assistants (PDAs), Personal Intelligent Communicators (PICs)—that are connected to a computing network in a wireless way are becoming popular. They typically have a non-continuous, low-bandwidth connection to the network. Mobile agents sent out from the mobile device into the network can do useful work in representing the mobile user. Time intervals in which the mobile device or the user is unreachable do not influence the processing of the roaming agent. As soon as the agent's task is accomplished and the mobile device is reachable, the agent returns with the results of its computation.

Even if there are no mobile devices with fragile network connections involved, mobile agents generally are a powerful computing paradigm because it may be cheaper and faster to move a data processing agent to the server where the data is located than to transfer back and forth many requests to the data over a possibly slow network. Specifically, queries that are not anticipated and prepared within a database are good candidates to be executed at the database server. The computation itself will be much more efficient if the requests to the data are processed locally at the server, i.e., the machine where the data is located. Of course, the tradeoff between moving the agent and moving the requests has to be taken into account. Sang et al. [Sang96] make comparisons of a mobile process approach with remote procedure call (RPC) and message passing solutions for parallel discrete event simulation. Their results show that the mobile process approach is more effective than RPC, and as efficient as message passing, with a major advantage being ease of model construction.

The more user-independent interaction there is between client and server, the more ef-

ficient it will be to move an agent representing the client to the server. For applications where data is accumulated and filtered by visiting a chain of servers, it may also be advantageous to employ an agent following this chain. It will return after successful completion with the resulting data; there is no need to move intermediate results to the client machine.

Today's computer networks often consist of hundreds or thousands of computers. Central control and monitoring of their operation is very difficult, if not impossible. One characteristic of such a network is its dynamics: machines are connected, disconnected, shut down, booted at arbitrary times. A group of mobile agents may be set up to watch locally for hot spots, bottlenecks, intruders and thus support the network manager.

The electronic marketplace is a major application area for mobile agents. Telescript, discussed later under Mobile Agent Systems, was mainly developed for this field. Mobile agents traveling through the internet or the World Wide Web look for the cheapest prices, make reservations, watch classified advertisements, and book theater tickets on behalf of their users.

Distributed problem solving in general is a domain for mobile agents. When the data to be processed is physically distributed, often central control is not feasible. Parallelism can be exploited by having several agents in the network to accomplish a complex task. They move around to combine the local data at the visited nodes, and they interact to exchange results and hints. The client-server paradigm is left, and the agents act as independent peers.

Design and Runtime System Requirements for Mobility

The engineering of mobile agent applications differs in several respects from that of static software components. Mobile agents leave their "home environment" and go to other environments in order to fulfill their task. This implies that the programmer of the mobile agent does not only have to take into consideration the home environment, but also all possible environments the agent may visit. Thus the set of imponderables and possible problems is much larger for mobile components. These problems can be reduced when care is taken that all sites have very similar environments, but having exactly the same environment everywhere is not feasible.

In general, the user or program that started the agent will not be available to help the agent when problems arise at a remote site. The non-local failure of an agent may be very difficult to detect.

This implies that the mobile agent must be able to work independently and asynchronously, and with a high resilience. It has to be a self-contained component that can interact flexibly with a number of (independently) developed components. This does not mean that it has to carry with it code for all of its possible actions. It should be a design goal to keep the agent as small as possible. The agent has to be able to fall back to a good infrastructure that provides the agent with additional functionality. This agent infrastructure is called the agent platform. It has to reside in each environment/site to which agents can travel.

An agent platform is similar to a componentware platform. In fact, it may be implemented as an extension to it. At the platform the supporting components must be present. The mobile agent can bind dynamically to these local (non-mobile) components. In order to keep the agent code itself small, a large part of the functionality has to reside outside the agent. If a certain expected functionality is neither part of the mobile agent, nor situated at the local platform, it may be dynamically loaded via the network.

How does a mobile agent platform differ from a componentware platform? Basically, the following extensions are needed:

- *Mobility:* packs, ships and unpacks mobile agents together with their accumulated program state. Mobility is invoked by the agent; the agent chooses when to move and where to go.

- *Vitality:* generates news agents, destroys obsolete agents.

- *Communication:* message exchange between agents. Sending messages to mobile agents is not as easy as to stationary components. They either have to be tracked, or messages have to be kept in a post-office mailbox.

- *Cooperation:* support agents that work on a common goal.

- *Dynamic loading:* to load new functionality that is needed locally by an agent.

In order to support mobility in heterogeneous environments, a mobile agent platform usually does not work with agents compiled to native machine code. Instead, interpreted languages or languages compiled to machine-independent byte-code are used. The byte-code compilation is used for efficiency and to hide the agent's program code from undesired readers.

Security is a major concern for mobile agent systems. Sites are not willing to accept agents that can do harm to the local data. Agent and sender identification and authentication concepts have to be incorporated. In addition, the agent's instruction set may be reduced at the receiving site to rule out access to nonpublic data. However, it is not only the receiving site that may be subject to an attack by the agent: the agent may also be attacked by the platform, exposing the agent owner's privacy—in an electronic commerce setting where an agent travels with the credit card number of its owner, the receiving site may scan the agent code for this number. Of course, there is a big difference between agent systems open for agents coming from all possible places, developed by an unknown programmer, and systems that are company internal and trusted.

Mobile Agent Systems

In this section we will review some of the existing mobile agent systems. We focus on systems that support autonomous mobility with accumulated state.

Intelligent Moving Processes (IMP). A forerunner of mobile code systems is the Intelligent Moving Processes (IMP) system [Wolfs89] developed by Siemens in the late 1980s. It provides the infrastructure that allows computer processes to move among heterogeneous computer systems. Program scripts are interpreted on the current machine until a "move" statement, which specifies a new machine to execute on, is reached. Executing the move statement causes state information and the program to be packaged and sent to the target machine. A dispatcher process on the target unpackages the state and causes execution to resume.

The interpreted scripts in IMP are arbitrary, parameterized subprograms written in a C-like language that contains primitives for interacting with the environment. Scripts can also execute at the operating system level. The Isis Distributed Toolkit is used as the underlying communication platform. Communication is possible via messages based on pre-defined message types. Agents are known by a unique name.

The initial application for IMP was controlling the flow of product through a factory [Voorh91]. More recently, the agents have been applied to the problem of managing information in large networks [Voorh94, Voorh94a].

Telescript. [White95] was developed by General Magic, a consortium of major players in the computer and telecommunication field. Telescript agents are written either in high- or low-Telescript. The high-Telescript language is object oriented and is compiled into byte-code (low-Telescript), which is interpreted by the Telescript engines. The unconventional syntax of high-Telescript may affect its acceptance. Agents migrate via the "go" command from one "place" to another, where they can "meet" other agents to communicate. This means that one agent can call the procedures of the other agent. Meetings are only possible between agents located at the same place; in order to meet a remote agent, the agent has to move. Besides the meeting construct, Telescript also provides non-local communication ("connect"), specifically for ongoing interaction between user and mobile agent. Agents posses descriptions of capabilities ("permits"), e.g., maximum lifetime and size. They can create other agents if they have the respective permit. A place offers services to the mobile agent. These services are stationary agents and may be written in C. Since Telescript is focused on the electronic marketplace, it will mostly be used for commercial services, e.g., a shopping center. Telescript has built-in persistency and safety (restricted access to system resources). These properties are very important to reduce the risks of failure and intrusion both for the agent and the places.

Agent Tcl. [Gray95] is being developed at Dartmouth College. The system is an extension of the widespread Tcl/Tk system, which is available on a large range of operating systems and machines. Both Tcl/Tk and Agent Tcl are interpreted languages. The agents are separate UNIX processes. They migrate from machine to machine using the "jump" command. Execution resumes on the destination machine at the statement immediately after the jump with the former accumulated state. In addition to migration, Agent Tcl supports message passing and direct connections (for bulk data transfer) between agents. Agents can make full use of the Tk facility to create graphical user interfaces on their current machine. For efficiency, parts of an agent may be written in C/C++, while stationary agents may be written completely in C/C++. Agents can create or clone agents. The current version supports only rudimentary security (it restricts connections to approved machines). Plans exists to add authentication and permits to increase security. Since the main features of Safe-Tcl [Boren94] will become part of the Tcl core, this functionality may be used, too. Multiple languages (Lisp, Java) and transport mechanisms will also be included. At Dartmouth College the system is currently used in information retrieval applications. Agent Tcl in the final version to come can be seen as an implementation of a big part of Telescript functionality, but based on more conventional languages.

Ara. [Peine95] also was heavily inspired by Telescript. Agents, which run as separate threads on a core, can "go" to other places, where they continue after the go statement with their accumulated state, and "meet" services announced by local agents. Ara supports Tcl and MAZE (a C++ intermediate interpretable byte-code). Security is planed based on Safe-Tcl concepts.

Tacoma. [Johan95] supports agents written in Tcl based on Horus/Isis for communication and fault tolerance. Agents can both move to other machines and communicate with other agents via the meet command. However, the state to be transferred has to be explicitly provided by the programmer by packing "briefcases." This makes programming less comfortable, but will in general reduce the size of state to be transferred. Basic security is provided by

accepting only agents coming from trusted hosts.

Hohl System. [Hohl95] uses Java as the base language for his mobile agent system. Agents move to other machines via the iWantToGoTo command. After migration, the agent does not continue with the statement following this call, but always with the start-method. The data to be transferred together with the agent code has to be specified in the program using a persistency manager.

Local communication between agents is done using a local procedure call. Both partners have to engage in a meeting before the initiator can call the procedures in the other agent. The meeting is necessary to prohibit movement during a communication. Non-local communication is possible via messages (if the location of the recipient is known) or via mailboxes.

This list of mobile agent systems is not by any means complete. Other systems exist with similar functionality and comparable concepts. Most of them—like most of the systems discussed above—are experimental systems for studying mobility as such; they are not designed with specific applications or application areas in mind. All systems support communication of agents, but none supports non-trivial cooperation protocols.

There is a clearly recognizable trend to extend existing languages and platforms, and not to invent new systems. Taking an interpreted language or a language compilable with byte-code as a basis is a requirement for achieving heterogeneity. (Stationary agents can be implemented in compiled C/C++ for efficiency in most systems.) The compilation to byte-code and the network awareness makes Java an ideal base system for mobile agents. Java is going to run on almost any system because the Java interpreter is integrated in popular web browsers. We expect to see more mobile agent systems based on Java in the near future.

Although many mobile agent systems exist, there are some open research problems.

- *Debugging:* How can a debugger follow a mobile agent through the network?

- *Management:* How can a system administrator manage agent societies?

- *Achievement of global goals:* Can performance be guaranteed, observed and controlled?

- *Security and agent privacy:* How can one prevent an agent from being inspected deeply by a remote site (e.g., to look for the owner's credit card number or favorite leather store)?

The Common Object Request Broker Architecture (CORBA) is an important component-ware platform. There exists a request for proposal [Virdh95] to integrate an agent facility to support mobile agents in the CORBA standard. As with CORBA itself, the concept is language-independent. Mobile agents have to be handled differently from normal CORBA objects. Agents are mobile objects that can move to other machines at their own will. Therefore, references to such an agent may be invalid and may have to be traced and updated in order to invoke the correct object server. Encoding should be compliant to the existing IDL (Interface Description Language). Naming should be location-independent, and agent names should be globally available. Location of agents in the distributed system should be possible via their name, their properties, and their capabilities. The RFP requests security concepts for runtime resource access security, i.e., items such as killing malicious agents, permissions, credit, etc.

The integration of a mobile agent concept would be a mayor step both for CORBA and for mobile agent technology. Mobile components would then be able to migrate to their server(s) and to their client(s) in the distributed system.

Cooperating Mobile Agent Systems and Swarm Intelligence

Mobile agents may accomplish their tasks either alone or in cooperation with others. Cooperative problem solving by agents is especially suited for decentrally organized systems. An example of cooperating mobile agents are cooperating "knowbots" searching in huge distributed search-spaces. They may share hints with strategic information and thus speed up the search process.

Cooperative problem solving by stationary software agents is a well established field [Hauge95]. By contrast, the field of cooperating mobile agents is just emerging. The main challenge for the system designer of cooperating mobile agents is the design of cooperation forms based on minimal or no communication. This is crucial, since mobile agents are often anonymous and have only a limited life span. For the definition of the desired cooperation methods, the Artificial Life (AL) research is very stimulating. The general objective of the AL-field is the simulation of biological processes either to understand them better or to build bionic systems, that is, technical systems that imitate natural behavior. A subfield of AL where both directions are pursued is what is called *Swarm Intelligence*.

Swarm Intelligence systems have the following characteristic: overall systems behavior is not explicitly programmed. It results from the behavior and the interaction of (relatively) simple agents. That is the reason why this approach is called Swarm Intelligence: the swarm of agents creates the problem solution. Biological swarm intelligence simulation demonstrates how insects cooperate without direct communication either exclusively by following a set of simple rules [Levy93] or by using chemical markers to lure others to the same spot (in order to work or to find food, for example [Deneu92]). These ideas inspired both work in experimental robotics [Thera92] and our own research into Swarm Intelligence problem solving based on a dynamic population of mobile software agents. Regulation strategies, which are also realized by software agents, enhance the realization of global objectives in a changing environment.

The main potential benefits of the Swarm Intelligence systems are:

- *Scalability/adaptability:* fast and automatic reaction to a pulsating problem size, for example, in load management scenarios by a dynamic agent population

- *Evolutionary extensibility:* efficient support when boundary conditions change—this may be realized using new types or versions of agents that replace dynamically the old ones

- *Robustness and smooth degradation:* realized by decentralized problem solution via a dynamic population of agents

An exemplary application scenario for Swarm Intelligence is the load management in telecommunication networks. Appleby [Apple94] describes such an application. Slightly simplified, there are two types of agents: mobile strategic agents and mobile load agents. The mobile strategic agents recognize load anomalies and initiate load agents to work for load producing nodes. Each load agent computes the currently optimal routing table for its node. Both agent types work concurrently. The size of the population of strategic agents depends on the size of the underlying network; the size of the population of the load agents depends on the severity of load anomalies. The main challenge of this scenario is the definition of ef-

ficient strategies, e.g. when and where to initiate the load agents. We used the basic ideas presented in Appleby [Apple94] to implement and evaluate ten different strategies. The implemented strategies fall into three classes:

- *Shortest path:* a static approach without agents—all connections are routed via the shortest paths in the network; there is no adaptation to the load

- *Best path:* dynamic strategies using mobile swarm agents which, in a distributed process, calculate the best routing for the current load—the strategies vary with respect to at which node and under which load conditions a mobile load agent is started

- *Alternative routing:* several routes may be used for different connections between two nodes—these different routes may either be pre-computed and further on remain fixed, or be dynamically adapted to the current load using swarm agents

Static strategies are of course not built to do any balancing dynamically. Within the dynamic *best path strategies,* the best performance is achieved when load agents are started at the node with the highest source rate. The number of load agents can be reduced significantly when the gradient of the load history of this node is taken into account. Alternative routing strategies tend to increase network load and to worsen load balancing because part of the connections are routed via nonbest paths.

In addition to balancing the load in the network, the dynamic strategies are able to cope with breakdowns of nodes and connections, since the routing tables are computed dynamically. Most of the implemented dynamic strategies are reactive, which means that they start to balance load only after anomalies have been noticed. Three proactive strategies have been implemented. They start load agents even if no anomalies have been detected. They significantly reduce load imbalances when sudden bursts of load appear. However, they show instabilities when the load balance is good. Currently we are combining the proactive with the reactive approach, and we integrate a learning module to recognize changes in the load that return regularly.

Conclusion

Mobile agents are an important extension of distributed component-based systems. Their task and location autonomy allows them to tackle complex problems in large networks. Cooperation in multi-agent systems makes them even more powerful. A number of systems are available already. However, they are either experimental or based on unconventional languages. The integration of a mobile agent facility into the componentware platform CORBA would be an important step. Robust mobile agent systems are expected in the near future, with Java being a base platform with high potential.

References

[Apple94] Appleby, S., Steward, S., Mobile Software Agents for Control in Telecommunication Networks, *BT Technology Journal,* 12(2), April 1994.

[Auer95] Auer, K., *Agents.* Central Queensland University Australia, available only at http://www.pcug.org.au/~kauer/project/main.htm

[Boren94] Borenstein, N., Email with a Mind of its Own: The Safe-Tcl Language for Enabled Mail. *Proceedings IFIP International Working Conference on Upper Layers Protocols, Architectures, and Applications (ULPAA),* Barcelona, 1994.

[Chess95] Chess, D., Grosof, B., Harrison, C., Levine, D., Parris, C., Tsudik, G., Itinerant Agents for Mobile Computing, *IEEE Personal Communications,* 2(5), 34–49.

[Deneu92] Deneuborg, J. L., Theraulaz, G., Becker, R., Swarm-Made Architectures. Towards a Practice of Autonomous Systems. *Proceedings of the First European Conference on Artificial Life,* 1992, 123–133.

[Frank96] Franklin, S. and Graesser, A., *Is It an Agent or Just a Program?: A Taxonomy for Autonomous Agents.* Institute for Intelligent Systems, University of Memphis, March 1996. Available at http://www.msci.memphis.edu/~franklin/AgentProg.html

[Gray95] Gray, R., Agent Tcl: A transportable agent system, in Mayfield, J., and Finin, T., (editors), *Proceedings of the CIKM Workshop on Intelligent Information Agents, Fourth International Conference on Information and Knowledge Management (CIKM 95),* Baltimore, Maryland, December, 1995.

[Harri95] Harrison, C., Chess, D., Kershenbaum, A., Mobile Agents: Are they a good idea? *IEEE Personal Communications,* 2(5), 34–49.

[Hauge95] Haugeneder, H., Steiner, D., Cooperating Agents: Concepts and Applications. *Agent Software,* 80–106, London, 1995.

[Hohl95] Hohl, F., Konzeption eines einfachen Agentensystems und Implementation eines Prototyps, (in German) *Diplomarbeit,* Nr. 1267, Universität Stuttgart, Germany, 1995.

[Johan95] Johansen, D., Renesse, R. van, Schneider, F., An Introduction to the TACOMA Distributed System, *Computer Science Technical Report* 95-23, University of Tromsø, Norway, June 1995.

[Knabe95] Knabe, F., *Language Support for Mobile Agents.* Thesis, CMU-CS-95-223, Carnegie Mellon University, Pittsburgh, Dec. 1995.

[Levy93] Levy, S., *Artificial Life: a Report from the Frontier Where Computers Meet Biology,* Vintage Books, 1993.

[Peine95] Peine, H., *An Overview of Mobile, Interacting Agents in the Ara System.* Universität Kaiserslautern, Germany, available electronically at http://www.uni-kl.de/AG-Nehmer/Ara/

[Sang96] Sang, J., Mascarenhas, E., Rego, V., Mobile-Process-Based Parallel Simulation, *Journal of Parallel and Distributed Computing,* 33(1), Feb. 1996, 12–23.

[SAML] The Software Agents Mailing List, maintained by Marc Belgrave, available electronically at http://www.ee.mcgill.ca/~belmarc/agent_faq.html#HDR6

[Thera92] Theraulaz, G., Goss, S., Gervet, J., Deneuborg, J. L., Task Differentiation in Polistes of Wasp Colonies: A Model for Self-Organizing Groups of Robots, *Proceedings of the 2nd International Conference on the Simulation of Adaptive Behavior,* 1992, pp. 346-355.

[Thoms95] Thomsen, B., Knabe, F., Leth, L., Chevalier, P.-Y., Mobile Agents set to work, *Communications International,* July 1995.

[Virdh95] Virdhagrisswaran, S., Mobile Agent Facility, *OMG Common Facilities RFP,* Nov. 1995.

[Voorh91] Voorhees, E., Using Computerized Routers to Control Product Flow, *Proceedings of the 24th Annual Hawaii International Conference on System Sciences,* 2, Jan., 1991, 275–282.

[Voorh94] Voorhees, E., Software Agents for Information Retrieval, *Working Notes of the AAAI Spring Symposium on Software Agents,* March 21–23, 1994, 126–129.

[Voorh94a] Voorhees, E., Agent Collaboration as a Resource Discovery Technique, in Yannis Labrou and Tim Finin (editors), *Proceedings of the CIKM Workshop on Intelligent Information Agents, Third International Conference on Information and Knowledge Management (CIKM 94),* Gaithersburg, Maryland, December 1994.

[White95] White, J. E., *Mobile Agents, General Magic Inc.,* Oct. 1995. Also in Bradshaw, Jeffrey (ed.), *Software Agents,* Menlo Park, California: AAAI Press/The MIT Press, 1996.

[Wolfs89] Wolfson, D., Voorhees, E., Flatley, M., Intelligent Routers, *Proceedings of the 9th International Conference on Distributed Computing Systems (DCS-9),* Newport Beach, CA, June 5–9, 1989, IEEE Computer Society Press, 371–376.

The authors are software engineers at Siemens AG, Corporate R&D, Munich. Hermann Ilmberger has developed programming, visualization, and debugging tools for parallel and distributed systems. Currently, his work focuses on the technology of mobile, cooperating software agents.

After working in the development team of the BS2000 mainframe operating system, Jürgen Schmitz was a member of the distributed systems group, focusing on microkernel architectures and fault tolerant computing. Currently, his interests are in the technology of mobile and cooperative software agents and their application.

Sabine Thürmel's current work has two foci: problem solutions and tools for parallel and distributed systems (e.g., based on the technology of mobile, cooperating agents); and the elaboration of future trends in software and engineering.

Toward Mass-Customized Information Systems

Nickolas Makrygiannis
nickolas@adb.gu.se

Abstract

For a long time we have experienced a shift from custom specific development to mass-production of information systems (IS). Domain modeling and object oriented techniques are overwhelming us with new methods and tools by which we can reduce costs and shorten time-to-market for delivered systems. Analogies to the automobile and the LEGO industry are presented as signposts to places where these goals can be achieved. Well-defined building blocks and standardized interfaces increase reusability and promote more effective system development procedures for given needs. However, IS are neither cars nor LEGO spacecrafts. The product of configuring their building blocks is highly associated to the organizational structure they will support. IS can be used to rearrange work settings and communication patterns, and thereby organizational structures. They provide their users with alternative ways to cooperate that lead to new needs and requirements. IS with these features will be called sociotechnical systems. As long as we are unable to predict all possible future requirements and as long as there are benefits in mass producing, we need to extend existing methodology with tools and methods for mass-customizing IS. Still, there are problems in building infrastructural pools of components, specifically for sociotechnical systems. This was shown during a pilot study conducted at a big Swedish IS vendor of defense systems. This paper will report on these problems as well as on some theoretical ideas on how to deal with them. Finally, I will sug-

gest prospects for future research on how component delineation and composition of components can be made in accordance with real world settings.

Introduction

Through all these years of information systems development, we have experienced a shift from custom engineering to mass-production of information systems. Theoretical and practical efforts that prevent the reinvention of the wheel have always been welcomed by the IS industry. Custom engineering has been associated with high costs and has exceeded time schedules for product delivery. At the same time, areas like domain modeling and OOT have benefited from increased IS developer attention to designing methods for cutting costs by reducing variety in system specifications; reducing maintenance costs; and shortening the time-to-market period. Building infrastructural pools of components based on domain knowledge, together with a good organization for reuse, could cut lead times and strengthen the competitiveness in the market [Griss93].

Vendors of complex information systems act as system integrators rather than as traditional system developers. Investing in infrastructures seems to be a promising IS strategy for the future. Although this trend appears sound, we must still be able to build IS of high quality and there are certain required specifications to be met and satisfied. IS enterprises still need to be designed for specific customer businesses. Infrastructural pools of components must therefore rely on and be built upon certain real-world requirements originating from real business needs. If this proves successful with IS vendors and their customers, a shift towards mass-customization of IS will be required and developers will be faced with the challenge of building generally applicable IT-infrastructural components with customer requirements in hand. This trade-off will introduce a number of problems, all connected with the general problem of how to fruitfully combine an infrastructural perspective and an enterprise-based approach to IS development. Indeed, how to deal with this problem is a problem in itself.

IS vendors need to adopt a holistic approach to mass-customization of IS. They should recognize the linkages between how the organizational work gets done and all the other aspects of the customer's organization, including the organizational structure. The ideal situation would be one in which components could be mass-produced while their couplings could be customized according to organizational structure.

One hypothesis, though not empirically proven in this paper, is that when a vendor delivers an IS to its customer, he also delivers a piece of the customer's organizational structure. This as a consequence of following the requirement specification, which often specifies data flows dependent on particular arrangements, such as the reporting hierarchy currently used by the organization. Enterprise-based information systems, by using infrastructural components, must be made insensitive to organizational arrangements. Also, rules must be developed specifying how clusters of reusable components can be structured and combined in accordance with organizational structure.

Project SEMLA

Project SEMLA is a collaboration between industry and the Department of Informatics in Göteborg University. The project aims to set up a theoretical and methodological framework for industrial development of complex information systems based on an architectural and infrastructural approach. The industrial half of this partnership already has a successful infrastructural history in building complex technical systems. They also want to write successful models for their sociotechnical systems. The university, on the other hand, has a history in enterprise-based systems—it wants to test whether the theory for enterprise-based systems (or certain species of it) can guide the construction of infrastructural pools of components.

During 1995, a pilot study was conducted by the industrial partner's organization to lay down a general outline for future project work within SEMLA. The study identified some problems that obstruct the process of building infrastructural pools of components and the successful reuse of them in different projects. Some ideas on how to approach these problems were also developed during this study.

This paper reports on our reactions to the problems identified during this study, partly by using the theory for enterprise-based systems as a theoretical framework. The central aim is to suggest what should be investigated before we begin to develop principles for building up infrastructural pools of components for sociotechnical systems.

Disposition

In the following sections I shall give a short presentation of the industrial partner's view on infrastructure and reuse and a general presentation of the concept of enterprise-based systems. I shall also give a short description of the pilot study conducted during 1995 and the problems identified, highlighting the theoretical issues raised during the study in light of these problems. Finally, I shall present the need for models, methods, and tools supporting domain and enterprise analysis, requirement elicitation, and systems specification. These should also support a definition of components and their composition rules that is based on real-world circumstances and the state of things in an enterprise's microlevel.

Presentation of the Field

CelsiusTech Systems
CelsiusTech is part of the Celsius Group, Sweden's largest defense industry group and one of the ten largest industrial groups in Europe. CelsiusTech specializes in advanced electronics and systems technology for a wide range of defense and civilian applications. Today, CelsiusTech is operationally organized as CelsiusTech Electronics and CelsiusTech Systems. Together, the two companies have some 2000 employees. The product range of our collaborator, CelsiusTech Systems, includes naval-command and weapons-control systems; land-based command and control systems for coastal defense, the army, and the air force; and civilian air-traffic control systems.

Early in the 80s, CelsiusTech experienced difficulties in developing new systems with existing technology. Every system was custom-built and there were few opportunities for reuse, although many individual functions were similar. Also, too many system developers were engaged in basic development work for specific projects.

A decision to develop in the Ada programming language, thereby promoting the object-oriented paradigm, resulted in a new methodology for systems development that is used today. The key concept in this methodology is modularity. Systems are built based on computer modules—basic software modules and communication products that fit together via standardized interfaces. The goal is to promote reuse by building software-program libraries that can be stored and accessed by different projects.

CelsiusTech Systems also tries to adopt an architectural approach to systems development. That means that general system properties, general requirements for hardware and software, and general developing principles for families of similar products (i.e., domain models[1]) are developed and described in what are called *architectures.* These architectures should guide the production of similar systems and thus might shorten their time to market.

The new system-development model is based on 2167A, an industry standard for the development of complex defense IS originally developed by the US Department of Defense (DoD). Many of the ideas behind this methodology are well described in a book written by Humphrey [Humph89].

Enterprise-Based Systems
Enterprise-based systems is a concept originally developed at the Department of Informatics in Göteborg, by M.-Å. Hugoson. He has developed the theoretical foundation of the concept and put it into practice in a number of Swedish enterprises [Hugos89]. Further research on this approach has been conducted by others [Pessi90], [Magou91], [Eriks94], [Pette94]. In project SEMLA, we are interested in investigating how this approach could be used to guide the development of infrastructural pools of components for building enterprise-based systems.

The purpose of enterprise-based systems is to serve decentralized organizations constituted by organizational parts (called areas

---

1. This discussion was suggested by work done within project DUR [DUR93] and by Palmer [Palme90].

of activity, [Makry93]), each of which has complete responsibility for its resources and is regarded as the best qualified to design and implement its own IT support. The organizational structure, the responsibility delineations, and the cooperation model used should guide the shaping of the IS structure, the demarcation of the IS subsystem boundaries, and the realization of subsystem interaction. The theory is best regarded as a guide to a structural design of decentralized IS rather than as another methodology for IS development.

In short, the theory proposes the development of a set of Autonomous Information Systems (AIS), each supporting a separate organizational unit (which could be a department, a process, or a division). The entire collection of AIS constitutes a decentralized IS. These systems are expected to be flexible and easily adaptable to changes in the organization, and they should not affect the organizational structure. In other words, they should not force the organization to adapt to a certain structure. To achieve these features, enterprise-based systems are designed with a focus on system delineation. The decentralized system structure would depend on how responsibilities are distributed throughout an enterprise and the cooperation structure adopted by the enterprise. The different responsibilities would form quite independent areas of activity while their corresponding AIS formed independent subsystems. Thus, every structural change within an organizational unit (demarcated by its responsibility span) would only affect the AIS owned by that unit.

In summary, then, one can say that the most crucial aspect of a successful implementation of this theory would be the definition of the areas of activity.

The delineation instrument used to demarcate the boundaries of the areas of activity is based on the real-world responsibility areas in the organization. One important constraint is that an area of activity must be functionally independent and insensitive (at least for a longer period of time) to information provided from another area of activity. In other words, every area of activity must be self-sufficient and independent when fulfilling its piece of work.

Research Approach

In order to find a suitable area in the Celsius organization that might profit from our knowledge in enterprise-based systems, and in order to peel off the problems already observed at the organization prior to the SEMLA project constitution, we conducted a pilot study divided into different activities:

1. We brought together IS architects at CelsiusTech Systems and spokesmen for the theory of enterprise-based systems at several workshops to discuss the different perspectives.

1. We collected reports describing the CelsiusTech Systems IS development procedures, the IS architectures for some application domains, and the organization's overall IS strategy.

1. We conducted several open-ended interviews at customer organizations as well as a number of semistructured interviews with CelsiusTech Systems project leaders and representatives who had architecture responsibles.

This paper only uses the results from the interviews with representatives from the developer's organization. The basic research approach applied is a theoretical argumentation based on an analysis of gathered material. The collection and analysis of data can be characterized as qualitative research and the interview technique is modeled on Patton's "Interview guide approach" [Patto90]. We have tried to analyze how the problems identified by those interviewed could be approached by borrowing ideas from the theory of enterprise-based _systems.

We chose semi-structured interviews for the following reasons: The developer organization is large and has developed many projects. We suspected that using open-ended interviews would produce results that were highly diversified and full of contradictions. The representatives interviewed had backgrounds in different kinds of projects, each of which provided different perspectives and experiences. By using semistructured interviews, we felt that we would be able to better control the range of answers given to us. In addition, the analysis process would be easier.

The Problems

Although the CelsiusTech organization has had many successful reuse projects to date, the study identified some problems that obstruct the process of building infrastructural pools of components and the successful reuse of them in different projects. The systems implemented are highly technical, and to use the words of Checkland [Check81], they belong to the category of hard systems. Without making any attempt to simplify or make light of the efforts employed[1] for their implementation, the systems were engineered to achieve solutions to given problems; both the functional and the organizational aspects of the requirements were clearly understood from the beginning. Project success could also be due to the good implementation of

---

1. We should keep in mind that these systems are highly technical and complex naval command and weapon control systems that involve truly complicated design and implementation efforts.

ideas from the theory of domain modeling as well as object oriented technology (OOT). However, some problems were identified in the interviews.

Conceptual Discrepancies

During the study it became clear that it was difficult to tell the difference between what should be perceived as application-specific products and what should be perceived as platform components. Moreover, the term *platform* was often mixed up with the term *infrastructure.* However, in both cases, there was a reference made to the infrastructural pool of components to be reused. The real problem is that concepts are perceived differently by different people in the developing organization. Some believe that applications can never be placed in an infrastructural base of components, while others believe that they should be part of the platform if they are reused a sufficient number of times.

It seems to be difficult to reuse an application if there are not any clear procedures for reuse. Applications can be reused by relying on the personal knowledge of certain people in the organization who know the application well and who know what minor modifications it may take to adjust the components to variations of requirements. That is, however, hardly a clear reuse procedure. Conceptual discrepancies have other effects as well. Sellers can be confused because they do not always understand the products they sell—they talk about products, while the developers talk about applications and platforms. Another problem is that customer requirements are often expressed in a different language than that used by the developer. Even though this is an old problem, not unique for this case, it still requires many translation efforts to produce system specifications. There should be a conscious method of action to develop components for the infrastructure and components for specific requirements. A formal organization for reuse should also be developed. All this requires that conceptual discrepancies can be discovered, diagnosed, and reduced to a level of consensus so that a group of actors can handle an activity less biased by misconceptions and misunderstandings.

Projects with a Life of Their Own

Another problem is that all the project teams have their own budget and time schedules to meet. This pressure discourages reuse. They do not have either the money or the time to develop for reuse. Thus, a vicious cycle is formed: A project with a restricted budget does not promote development of components that can be reused. A second project, equally pressed, has nothing to reuse or is unaware of what can be reused from the first project. The second project does not have the time to develop components that could be reused either, and the circle is well under way. The situation could benefit from the development of tools for browsing existing components. But this would require that there be a clear conceptual agreement about what a component is.

Low Support for Reuse

The most articulated need during the interviewing was the urgent need for a general and company-common platform to rely on when starting a project: developers do not have tools or procedures to apply in order to find assets developed elsewhere in the organization that can be reused. The absence of such a common platform also impedes the development of open architectures, which causes integration problems with Components on the Shelf (COTS).

Defective Documentation of Architectures

The systems developed by the development organization are rigorously documented according to project and system documentation rules recommended by the 2167A standard. On the other hand, the general system-development philosophy is not equally well documented. Rules for what should be regarded as general components and what should be regarded as application-specific components are also badly documented. Products developed at different places in an enterprise are not easy to find. Too much tacit knowledge is built in the "walls" and in the personal knowledge of a few people. How can this knowledge be known and distributed? How can it be documented?

Inflexibility in Meeting Requirements

Although there are some problems with integrating products developed in-house with external COTS, it is theoretically possible. But this could result in solutions that are inflexible to the customer. The customers risk being tied to the developer in a way that is not desirable. In the long run, this can mean deteriorated competitiveness for the developer.

Problems associated with mass-production sometimes make it difficult for the developer to meet specific requirements. This often causes several negotiation meetings to take place between developers and customers to modify or respecify requirements so they can be met by in-house knowledge and/or existing products.

Discussion

During the pilot study, we interviewed representatives experienced in the development of naval- as well as land-based command systems. Both involve high technology and high technical-development skills and both can be regarded as hard systems with sociotechnical parts. However, I shall make a distinction between these two categories in order to illustrate the importance of paying greater attention to organizational aspects when developing infrastructural pools of components. Naval-command systems were developed as hard systems, which made it difficult to reuse the enterprise-oriented parts of the platform developed for other application domains such as land-based command systems. And the latter, which in many respects uses similar systems, was nevertheless not easy to develop based on components from the naval platform

I would claim that part of the reason for this was that the organizational structure supported by land-based command systems was different from that supported by naval command systems.

Explaining the Success of the Naval-Command System

When conducting the study at CelsiusTech Systems, we could discern a more optimistic attitude among the representatives for the naval systems towards applying the company's systems-development methodology. Their satisfaction in the use of an infrastructure of reusable components and a common platform was obvious. In fact, the representatives felt that their success was almost entirely due to this approach for dealing with the development of a set of ordered systems. On the other hand, representatives for the land-based systems pointed out that the lack of such a common platform was a problem.

The success of the naval systems–development methodology could also have been due to the fact that the application domain for this kind of system became very well understood as a number of orders came in during the same period of time. The ordered systems were complex, technical systems

and their properties could easily be explained and mediated between customers and vendors.

Another reason for their success could be that these orders necessitated the development of a common platform just to rationalize the process of building a number of similar systems in a short time. Components were developed that could be reused with modest modifications between the applications. The identified problem of not having the time to build components for reuse was not present here. In addition, the requirements concerning the functionality of the components were apparently clearly understood and no misconceptions occurred.

Furthermore, the naval-system success could be ascribed to the fact that people who were engaged in many of the projects conveyed tacit (architectural) knowledge about how these systems should be built. In that way the urgent need for documentation of products, components, composition rules, component delineations, and architectures was not obtrusive.

Despite their success, enterprise-oriented components from the naval-command–systems domain could not be reused with the same success in the domain of land-based–command systems because the development approach for these components was more technically oriented. To increase reuse and spread the success of this method to other domains as well, a sociotechnical approach should be applied. The organizational aspects are very important in the design of sociotechnical systems. These systems support organizations full of people, with certain responsibilities and roles, who perform activities that are nested in a cooperational network much dependent on the organizational structure. These organizational aspects have to be taken into account in the development of component infrastructures.

Hard vs. Sociotechnical Systems

Every organizational system has a structure, defined by the couplings between its various parts. Checkland [Check81] describes organizational structure in terms of of the reporting hierarchy, the power structure, the communication pattern, or the physical organizational layout.

Different organizations may belong to the same domain, but they may differ in structure. One can be hierarchically organized while another is a network, despite the fact that they may both produce the same products or provide similar services.

The difference between hard systems (e.g., naval- and weapons-control systems and sociotechnical systems) is that in hard systems the structure is more or less given. The information flow and the usage of information are given, as are the functions that are performed. How an anti-aircraft gun on a battleship should act after a certain signal has been provided to it is rigidly predetermined. Therefore the situation cannot, and should not, be compared to a situation in which a human gets a piece of data that must be interpreted and probably passed on to another human for further interpretation or to provide a basis for a certain action. Such a chain of "interpretators," connected by the information flow, can change and adapt. And today, with the help of IT, it can do so more easily!

The major source of the first problem identified in the study has to do with discrepancies in how different people conceptualize the things that really matter in a certain situation. The difficulty in analyzing and specifying requirements is present regardless of the kind of system asked for. However, I claim that it is more difficult when the resulting system is to be of a sociotechnical kind. Requirements are strictly formulated for hard systems; they are given.

In sociotechnical systems, they are always changing and so there is a great risk that they will be misinterpreted. We all know that there are many examples of systems implementations where the products do not satisfy the needs of their human operators even though they are technically sound.

Supported by Dobson and Strens [Dobso94], I claim that technical solutions to problems are often created in ways that do not adequately support the way in which the human components of the work system are organized. Sociotechnical systems are systems that are placed in a social context and have the ability to affect this context. This ability is the main thing that makes them different from hard systems. Creating infrastructural pools of components for building systems of this kind is associated with different problems and needs a different approach than just mass-producing components and fixed interfaces between them. However, I believe that pools of components could still be built if we could find a way to separate the structural aspects of an organization from its functional aspects.

Earlier I suggested that IS vendors, when delivering an IS, also deliver a piece of the customer's organizational structure. The design effort of the IS vendor risks cementing the currently used cooperation model—which is the structure—between people, roles and activities performed within the customer's organization if there is a high concentration on technical and economic aspects when designing the system structure. Our study showed that systems are often configured in a certain way either because it is technically appropriate or because it is easier to market a cheaper system constituted by less hardware. However, there is a risk that solutions of this kind will bind up different organizational units in a way that obstructs future need for organizational changes.

Enterprise-Based Systems and the Microlevel

Every structure can be divided in two parts: an inner structure (a micro level) and an outer structure (a macro level).

When building enterprise-based systems, the IS macrolevel boundaries are determined and set on the basis of the responsibility span of each area of activity— i.e., the organization's structural counterparts. Every AIS forms a macrostructural part or else a part of the outer structure. Every AIS is loosely coupled to the other AIS in order to preserve real-world independence between the areas of activity.

The very strength of enterprise-based systems is their conformity to the real-world settings in the enterprise. The system structure mirrors the actual organizational structure and is designed to ensure organizational changes. Systems are small; they are flexible; they are not dependent on each other; they can be implemented on different platforms and they are open to cooperate with other systems. In other words, they provide the characteristics that we wish were exhibited by our infrastructural components.

Figure 1 illustrates the level of abstraction addressed by the concept of enterprise-based systems (together with many other concepts presented in this paper). It can be seen that the macrolevel (i.e., the department level) has nothing to do with the internal structuring or development of the microlevel components. Every AIS can, in a sense, be regarded as a macro-component. However, it should also address the micro-component level as well.

Thus, the main question is what is the particular delineation instrument rooted in the enterprise microlevel that could be used to make the inner structure as enterprise-based as the outer structure? What is a suitable abstraction level for the microlevel? What should we use as the real-world base for the delineation of the infrastructural components? What is the lowest level of structurally independent organizational functions?

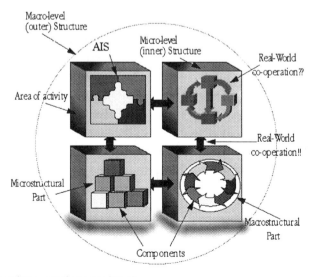

Figure 1. Illustration of the micro- and macrolevel.

Structures and Cooperation

The degree of integration and independence between the parts in an organizational structure is set up by the structure. The cooperation between the parts reflects the structure. If the structure changes, so does the cooperation model applied between the parts. We need information systems easily adaptable to such changes, because when changes occur in the cooperation model between organizational parts, this results in changed demands on the supporting information system.

On the other hand, information systems are also constituted of parts interrelated to each other in an IS structure. Parts of an IS, like areas of activity, cooperate in order to fulfill their respective function (even though they often cooperate to complement each others functions rather than to fulfill their own). Every part of an IS always has a boundary that delineates its inner structure from the IS outer structure. To determine that boundary is not always easy if we do not use an agreed-upon delineation instrument telling us what a part is and what it is not.

In change situations, the inner structural parts often tend to swell in a way that blurs the original boundary settings against both macrostructural and other microstructural parts of the structure. Uncontrolled growth of this kind can create dependencies, not only within the system, but also in the enterprise it serves.

Component boundary setting is a highly important design issue and it should be related to the enterprise microlevel settings. Composing components is an equally important issue: to base it solely upon technical suitability or economical premises is to disregard the organizational context.

However, there is a difference between cooperation between areas of activity on the one hand and, on the other, the subsystems or components in a certain IS. Too often, area-of-activity cooperation needs are treated as a subsystem of component cooperation needs. The result is that this business cooperation is embedded in the system because this is often considered the technically proper way to satisfy these needs. For example, to support the operational cooperation needs between two separate (and for the case of the example, highly independent) areas of activity by means of a shared IS could be technically and economically defensible, but the solution would be too restrictive for the two involved areas since their real-world business activities would be functionally dependent on each other. And this dependence would be caused by the implemented IS. It would be more proper to partition the database used by these two areas or even to put them in two different computers. Cooperation between areas of activity should be mediated by the system, not embedded in it [Makry95].

We have stressed the importance of conformity between the IS structure and the organizational structure, and recognized the importance of having a flexible IS structure because organizational changes are common. But flexibility should be present at all system levels, both macro and micro.

We have also claimed that the cooperation model, i.e., the way information flows within an organization, is governed by organizational structure. That means that it is sensitive to organizational changes. The IS structure should support these changes, which means that the IS structure should be flexible enough to support different organizational structures.

I would like to stress the importance of finding ways to model enterprises in a way that makes a distinction between functions performed and cooperation between enterprise parts down to the microlevel.

Dobson and Strens [Dobso94] make a useful distinction between organizational requirements and functional requirements. Organizational requirements are defined as those that come out of a system placed in a social context rather than those that derive from functions to be performed or tasks to be assisted. Examples of sources of such requirements are power structures, obligations and responsibilities, control, and autonomy. These are embedded in the organizational structure. They suggest that an organization should be perceived as a network of responsibilities that embody aspects of structure as well as function. The users' real requirements are manifest in the responsibilities they hold in that they have a need to know things, a need to do things for the proper fulfillment of their responsibilities, and a need for audit in order to show how they have fulfilled their responsibilities.

Dobson and Strens work in a research group at the University of Newcastle that has produced the ORDIT methodology. One of the main characteristics of the ORDIT approach is that it models responsibilities and relationships rather than activities [Dobso92], [Pouls92], [Dobso93]. This approach can contribute to a better understanding of what could be regarded as purely functional components; what could be regarded as context-dependent components; and what the composition rules should be based on—and could give us a clue about how a suitable enterprise model would look.

Conclusions

The necessary prerequisite for developing enterprise-based information systems based on an infrastructural pool of components is that the design of components must be done with no regard to organizational structure. Components must not embed any structural aspects of the organizational arrangements. The component composition rules have to be designed in accordance with the real-world arrangements in the organization's microlevel. In other words, we should investigate the possibility of designing micro-components insensitive to organizational context. We should be looking for a delineation instrument supporting component delineation that makes them insensitive to the way an enterprise could be structured. The component should support an act of work, not an act of cooperation. So, even though we do not yet know the characteristics of those components, we propose that they must be designed independently of things that have to do with organizational structure.

Making clusters of components sensitive to a certain organizational structure requires a set of composition rules that implement the cooperation model in the actual organization. Cooperation models are models of the communication pattern, the reporting structure, and the power hierarchy, as described by Checkland [Check81]. Since these entities are expressions of the organizational context, they should be left out of the implementation of the physical IS components. Clusters of IS components can never constitute an IS as long as the components are not tied together in a network specified by the organizational structure. The IS components are defined by functional requirements and designed to support functions, processes, or specific tasks that are needed to support an organization's objectives—i.e., the job that has to be done.

Suggested Research Areas

Developers are faced with the challenge of meeting the customer's specific needs while at the same time focusing on building and using an infrastructural base of IT components. They are also faced with the challenge of using these very needs to:

- Find and reuse existing components

- Determine what composition rules should be applied

- Define, delineate, and design new components

- Define and design rules for composing components according to the given requirements.

The prerequisite to all this is that developers, as well as customers, have methods and tools in hand to analyze the enterprise; to elicit and specify requirements; and to express and understand needs in a way that is suitable for their purpose.

Of course, this leads us to emphasize the necessity, if not of a common language, at least of a method that will reduce the impact of misunderstanding between actors involved in the system-development cycle. Too many problems exist, specifically in the requirement elicitation and analysis phase, where discrepancies in communication lead to systems badly customized to real-world requirement needs. Thus, the *first* suggested research effort should address questions like: Can discrepancies be discovered, diagnosed, and reduced to a level of consensus so that a group of actors can handle an activity less biased by misconceptions and misunderstandings? Is there a method for diagnosing discrepancies, and are there ways to reduce them?

If we could handle this Tower of Babel in system development, we would, in the long run, gain increased efficiency and reduced costs and be able to develop information systems that can more accurately respond to given requirements.

We have discussed the necessity of an approach for analysis and requirement elicitation that takes into account that IS are systems that are placed in a social context and affect this context. IT can be used to rearrange work setting, communication patterns, and organizational layout, and hence the organizational structure. Developers must recognize this in their efforts to build up IT infrastructural

components and composition rules for building IS of this kind.

Thus, a *second* suggested research effort should address questions like: How can an enterprise be understood and analyzed in terms of activities, tasks, or functions that can be rearranged in different networks according to structural changes? Related questions are: Is there a way to mediate enterprise descriptions and user needs in a terminology adopted and understood by all the involved parties? Can this same terminology be used for different purposes, i.e., to provide customers with an instrument for expressing their needs and provide developers with an instrument to design components and component composition rules? What existing theories and methodologies (e.g., enterprise-based systems, ORDIT) could be used to help achieve this?

Conducting the above-described research should provide us with a delineation instrument, based on real-world circumstances and the state of things in an enterprise's microlevel (i.e., activity and task level), that could be used to define and design software components insensitive to changes in organizational structure.

Thus, a *third* research effort should address question like: What characterizes an insensitive component? Can we design components in direct conformity with the real-world circumstances and state of things in an enterprise's microlevel? How do we design components to make them applicable in organizations with a different structure? What existing methodologies (e.g., OOT, domain modeling) could contribute to this research effort?

The ability to build systems that satisfy given properties from a selected set of specified components is a prerequisite for the production of networks, the production of systems using COTS, and the production of systems from verified components. However, this presupposes a theory of system composition. The composition of components must be governed by the composition of the enterprise activities or the functions supported by the components. They must be composed in accordance with the cooperation model used in the real-world settings.

Thus, a *fourth* research effort should address questions like: What is a composition rule? What is its real-world counterpart in the organization? How do we define and design composition rules? What coupling do they have to specified components? When do we apply a rule? Is there a method to be used for this purpose? Additional questions will probably be generated by the research efforts described above.

Our study showed that discrepancies in terminology also occur between different developer teams or project teams working in the same group. Unless certain people carry knowledge with them between the different projects, developers do not always know what components have been designed, where they can be found, or if they can be reused in the first place. Documenting how components and composition rules should be designed, as well as documenting existing components in the infrastructural base and existing composition rules, should be highly prioritized. Tools should also be constructed supporting the browsing of components and the rules in order to find the needed items to apply for meeting the requirements.

Models, tools, and method that can guide us in the analysis process so that we can distinctly elicit requirements that have to do with functions and those that have to do with structure are highly desirable. The product of applying these methods could, for example, be a chart of functional requirements (activities or tasks to be supported) that are clearly separated from structural aspects of the organization.

The functional requirements could, for instance, be targets for the design of insensitive components to fill up the infrastructural pool of components. The structural aspects could be the basis for designing rules for integrating these components in order to make clusters of components sensitive to the specific organization.

Acknowledgments

This research could not have been conducted without the invaluable help of numerous people at CelsiusTech Systems. Thanks to all who participated in our interviews and workshops. Thanks to Håkan Enquist for his helpful discussions analyzing the gathered material. Thanks also to Bo Dahlbom for his time discussing the presented material and Kjell Mellberg for reviewing the content. The research documented in this paper is a product of the SEMLA project. The project is partially funded by the Swedish National Board for Industrial and Technical Development (NUTEK). All possible errors in this paper naturally remain the responsibility of the author.

References

[Check81] Checkland, P., *Systems Thinking, Systems Practice,* New York, John Wiley & Sons Ltd., 1981.

[Dobso92] Dobson, J.E., Blyth, A.J.C., Chudge, J., and Strens, M.R., The ORDIT approach to requirements identification, *Proceedings of the 16th Annual International Computer Software and Applications Conference,* Sept 21–25, Chicago, Illinois, 356–361, 1992.

[Dobso93] Dobson, J.E., Blyth, A.J.C., Chudge, J., and Strens, M.R., ORDIT: A new methodology to assist in the process of eliciting and modelling organisational requirements, *Proceedings on the Conference on Organizational Computing Systems,* November, San Jose, California, 1993.

[Dobso94] Dobson, J.E. and Strens, M.R., Organizational requirements definition for information technology systems, *Proceedings of the IEEE International Conference on Requirements Engineering (ICRE94)*, IEEE Press, Colorado Springs, Colorado, April, 1994.

[DUR93] Telub Teknik et. al., Samarbetsprojekt IT4 , DUR: Datorstödd Utvecklingsmetodik för Rationella Informationssystem, Slutrapport, Telub Teknik AB, 1993.

[Eriks94] Eriksson, O., *Informationssystem med verksamhetskvalitet, Utvärdering baserat på ett verksamhetsinriktat & samskapande perspektiv*, Licentiate Thesis, Departments of Computer Science, Linköping Univeristy, 1994.

[Griss93] . Griss, M. L, Software reuse: from library to factory, *IBM Systems Journal*, 32(4), 1993, 548–66.

[Hugos89] Hugoson, M.-A., *A System of Systems: A Theory of Information System Architecture and Interaction*, Department of Computer Sciences, Chalmers University of Technology and the University of Gothenburg, 1989.

[Magou91] Magoulas, T. Pessi, K., *En studieom informationssystemarkitekturer*, Licentiate Thesis, Gothenburg Studies in Information Systems, report 2, Chalmers University of Technology and Göteborgs University, 1991.

[Makry93] Makrygiannis, N., *Integration and independence aspects on dispersed information systems*, Licentiate Thesis, Departments of Informatics, Chalmers University of Technology and the University of Gothenburg, 1993.

[Makry95] Makrygiannis, N., Dispersed information systems Struvtures: toward a balance between integration and independence, *Proceedings of IRIS 18, Design and Context, Part 2*, 451–464, 1995.

[Palme90] Palmer, C. and Cohen, C., Engineering and application of reusable software, *Journal of American Institute of Aeronautics and Astronautics*, 1990.

[Pessi90] Pessi, K., Strategier för strukturering av verksamheters Informationssystem, *Proceeding of Nordata 90*, 1990.

[Patto90] Patton, M. Q., *Qualitative Evaluation and Research Methods*, SAGE Publications.

[Pette94] Pettersson, K., *Informationssystemstruktur-ring, ansvarsfördelning och användar-inflytande, –En komparativ studie med utgångspunkt i två informationssystemstrategier*, Licentiate Thesis, Departments of Computer Science, Linköping Univeristy, 1994.

[Pouls92] Poulson, D.F.,Oswald, G., Chudge, J.S., and Strens, M.R., Modeling organisational complexity using the Ordit framework, *IEE International Conference on Information Decision ActionSystems in Complex Organisations Publication Number 353*, April 6–8, Oxford, England, 70–74, 1992.

[Humph89] Humphrey, W.S., Managing the software process, *SEI Series in Software Engineering*, Addison-Wesley Publishing, New York, 1989.

Department of Informatics, Göteborg University, Sweden.

Component-Based Systems
The Basis of Future Manufacturing Systems

John Edwards, Paul Clements, Jack Gascoigne, and Ian Coutts

Abstract

This paper discusses the requirements for next generation manufacturing software systems. It takes a component-based approach identifying the need to create dynamic systems that have a potential for continual change.

The paper describes the advances in object technology, distribution technology, and component software cooperation through semantic integration. It proposes a vision of next-generation manufacturing software systems based on these technologies and concludes that a complete solution to the problems of semantic integration is needed.

Manufacturing Enterprise Agility

Today's manufacturing companies are focusing on enterprise agility to enable them to react more quickly than their competitors to changing market needs. This does not necessarily imply wholesale reengineering, but it does imply a very rapid IT system development cycle or, even better, a system based on continual change, which can be adapted or which adapts itself to the needs of the enterprise on a day-by-day or hour-by-hour basis. It can be argued that this requirement can be satisfied by IT systems based on self-contained components that can be mixed and matched on an ad hoc basis to provide support for the business goals of an enterprise.

One of the main barriers to the implementation of agile systems has been the availability of suitable IT support technology. Advances in the key areas of object technology and distribution technology have begun to provide a basis for this new approach. The addition of solutions to the problem of object or component interoperation or cooperation could complete the picture. This paper highlights the need for further work in the area of semantic integration, which could provide a solution to component cooperation. The paper is based on the early findings of a UK government-supported project to identify and examine issues associated with the creation of agile systems.

Object Orientation

Current manufacturing systems have generally been created using the traditional software engineering paradigm, which typically produces centralized, functionally decomposed, monolithic, hierarchical software. However, this approach has not provided support for the dual demands of increased productivity and flexibility in software engineering. Neither is the same top-down philosophy likely to provide solutions to the problems of creating agile manufacturing systems, as the lengthy process from business analysis to system implementation can take years from initial modeling work to system hand-over.

Object orientation has long been championed as the solution to these problems. Recently there appears to be a change in attitude on the part of of those willing to adopt object technology. "…the fear of a new untested technology which apparently had little more than marketing hype to back its claims has been gradually replaced by an acknowledgment that object technology is likely to dominate software development by the turn of the century" [O'Call95].

The object paradigm incorporates a number of concepts that support flexibility—typically encapsulation, inheritance, polymorphism, and late binding. Encapsulation is almost certainly the most important; it allows an object to manage a resource of its own, access or use of this resource being controlled by the object through its own published interface. Objects can therefore provide some service to other objects while hiding all unnecessary detail from the user objects. This notion of encapsulation supports the requirement that agile systems comprise sets of self-contained components that combine with each other through using and offering services but have no need for detailed knowledge of each other's internal operations.

Object Distribution

A distributed system comprising a heterogeneous range of elements possibly spread around the world in a virtual enterprise must appear to the user as a single system. Users and applications should be able to interact with any resource without worrying about considerations such as protocols or transport medium. Orfali, Harkey, and Edwards conclude that distributed object technology provides the only realistic solution to distributed IT systems [Orfal]. The World Wide Web is proving to be another serious candidate.

The benefits of distributed object technology were recognized by the IT community in 1989 when the Object Management Group (OMG) was founded. Their original mission was to enable distributed transparent interaction between objects via an Object Request Broker (ORB).

In simple terms, the request broker architecture provides access mechanisms for application objects to a set of common services that support the needs of objects that must collaborate. A set of common facilities provides higher level services of both a general nature and an application domain-specific nature.

The OMG approach aims at common standards for object distribution, but unfortunately these are not common to Microsoft, who, of course, occupies a very significant part of the software marketplace. Their own solution to the problem—OLE/COM (Object Linking and Embedding/Component Object Model)—essentially provides a very similar set of common services that allows objects to collaborate (though currently only on single platforms). Only time will tell which technology will prevail, but in the meantime it remains a major headache for vendors and users attempting to migrate to a distributed object approach.

Component Systems

Software objects in standard object-oriented applications exist within a single program. Only the language compiler knows of their existence, and all their beneficial properties of encapsulation, inheritance, etc., are lost when they become a piece of compiled object code. A distributed object is a more sophisticated entity that can exist anywhere on a network. It is essentially autonomous and can be used by remote client entities invoking its advertised methods. The technology used to create and execute individual distributed objects is (or needs to be) irrelevant to individual objects working together in a system.

As such, distributed objects are software components that can be used as building blocks of distributed systems and can be viewed as the "software ICs" that Brad Cox introduced as long ago as 1987 [Cox87]. To continue Cox's analogy, the software printed circuit board into which his software ICs can be plugged may be termed a "framework" in that it can follow a standardized, or at least a generally accepted, form.

The framework and component approach offers many benefits to users, vendors and systems builders but it is not the ultimate goal. Fully cooperating components collaborate at a semantic level, enabling components with no prior knowledge of each other to work together. The technology for achieving semantic integration is currently undergoing extensive research and forms an important part of the work at MSI.

A Vision of Future System Creation, Use, and Maintenance

A solution enabling full component cooperation will empower users to build and rebuild their systems on the fly. In his column for the *Object Expert Journal,* Jean Marie Chauvet quotes a recent study by the analyst group Hambrecht and Quist [Chauv96]. The summary of IT trends in the study focuses on the empowerment of the end user and the reformulation of application software. Chauvet explains that the unleashing of end-user demand for information and task automation manifests itself in a reformulation of application software from a small number of monolithic, centralized, large programs to thousands of specialized tactical applications, specifically targeted to individual or work group needs.

Taken to its logical conclusion, staff within a manufacturing enterprise could select the most appropriate set of tactical application objects or components suited to the requirements of their task for the day (or hour). These components could include "thin" clients accessing servers running on platforms on the other side of the world. The users could configure their components to form a working system via their personal desk top, use the system to achieve their goals, and destroy the system to clean up and make ready for their next task.

Semantic Integration

Semantic integration holds the key to component cooperation. A complete solution will enable components with no prior knowledge of each other to communicate in a meaningful and open manner in order to accomplish some desired goal. This section introduces four of the main players in distributed object technology—namely, the Object Management Group, CI Labs, the Intelligent Agent community, and the SSA—and discusses how their approach covers transparent component distribution facilities (requisite A) and communication of knowledge between components (requisite B), two of the key requirements for semantic integration.

The Object Management Group— CORBA

The OMG was formed in 1989 by 11 member companies and has grown to over 600 participating members with the aim of promoting the theory and practice of object technology for the development of distributed computer systems. Central to the OMG concept is their Object Management Architecture (OMA) which "identifies and characterizes the components, interfaces and protocols that compose the OMA but does not in itself define them in detail." The main components of the OMA are:

- *An Object Request Broker (ORB),* which enables and manages the distribution of objects
- *Object Services,* which provide the means for managing the life cycle of the objects

- *Common Facilities,* which provide a generic set of services useful to all users

- *Application Objects,* which cover components that are specific to the end-user applications

In terms of the ability to meet requisite (A), OMG has CORBA, which provides a comprehensive set of services that can enable and manage the distribution of objects over a variety of platforms and operating systems.

In terms of the ability to meet requisite (B), OMG uses vertical domain task forces to create application objects built upon the underlying defined OMG services, the Manufacturing Task Force being one example. Recently, it has complemented this with a request for a proposal for Common Business Objects (CBOs) and a Business Object Facility (BOF). The BOF is a standard software infrastructure that is required to support business objects at runtime as "plug and play" application components. Here "plug and play" implies that business objects will be able to work together within some standard framework; it does not imply that components with no prior knowledge of each other (or any standard that each other might comply with) can cooperate.

CI Labs—OpenDoc

CI Labs was formed in 1993 by eight member companies with the aim of promoting, establishing and certifying OpenDoc and related compound document technologies. Central to the OpenDoc architecture are:

- A means for distributing the objects

- Document management

- The ability to coordinate the actions of various OpenDoc components

In terms of the ability to meet requisite (A), OpenDoc specifies use of IBM's System Object Model (SOM), which is a CORBA-compliant ORB.

In terms of the ability to meet requisite (B), CI Labs offer the ability to ensure that components that are labelled as OpenDoc components do comply to the OpenDoc specification. Co-ordination between OpenDoc components is defined through the use of a scripting language. This approach provides an advanced form of component system building, but again the technology falls short of the ultimate goal.

With regard to OLE/COM, CI Labs have developed a technology called Component-Glue to enable OpenDoc components to collaborate with OLE-based components.

SSA—NEWI

The NEWI product, marketed by SSA, is not primarily aimed at manufacturing systems, but it provides a good example of how some of the semantic integration issues can be tackled. It allows the definition of fully encapsulated business objects which, individually, provide a part of the functionality available in a system to a user. In terms of the ability to meet requisite (A), a separate, infrastructural, element provides for the mechanism of interaction between these components. The fact that this infrastructure is particular to NEWI is a potential drawback.

In terms of the ability to meet requisite (B), definitions of member data of NEWI objects is done in such a way as to enable components to request information—e.g. first_name—from another component. The key to this is that the receiving object controls this activity; hence the data-providing object needs no knowledge of the receiver concerning what it does or what parameters it will require. In general terms, objects are built with no inherent precoded knowledge of the other objects with which they will subsequently interact.

For meaningful interaction, to fulfil some system goal, knowledge about which objects should interact and when they should interact must exist somewhere. With NEWI, this is primarily supplied by the user via manipulation of visual objects, each related to an underlying business object. Thus the "which and when" is defined distinctly from the "how and what."

Obviously, such an approach is more suited to a completely "human-serving" process such as a query desk than, say, an automated manufacturing cell. There are two answers to this:

1. There are many situations in a purely manufacturing solution context where this could be applied directly for at least part of the solution.

1. The possibility exists for providing the desired interaction definitions from a nonhuman source—i.e., defined as part of the system configuration.

This latter approach means that an IT system would be seen as a collection of potentially interacting components whose specific interactions can be rapidly defined and re-defined, possibly even by the end users.

Intelligent Agent Community— KIF/KQML

The technologies previously described have primarily been driven by commercial organizations, whereas currently the technologies associated with creating and using intelligent agents exist in the academic domain. Of particular interest in this paper is the work taking place under the umbrella of the Knowledge Sharing Effort (KSE) sponsored by ARPA in the US.

The primary goal of the KSE is to enable the representation and sharing of knowledge between knowledge bases. They have identified four distinct working groups to consider

pertinent issues within knowledge representation:

- Developing a common language for expressing the content of the knowledge base

- Developing the ability to define common constructs within families of representation languages

- Facilitating consensus on shared knowledge within particular topic areas and topic-independent areas

- Creating runtime interaction between knowledge bases and other systems

In terms of the ability to meet requisite (A), the group has defined an agent-communication language known as KQML (Knowledge Query and Manipulation Language) that defines a set of "performatives" (similar to services). This provides a means for intelligent agents to describe their needs and capabilities to other intelligent agents, which allows agents to interact in an ad hoc manner.

In terms of the ability to meet requisite (B), KSE has defined a formal representation known as KIF (Knowledge Interchange Format) that allows the developer to describe knowledge in a formal, computer-understandable manner.

The main advantage of this approach is that it enables agents to operate in an autonomous manner but, when the need arises, to also issue a KQML message asking for some capability, not caring who provides it; other agents can determine whether they can provide the capability.

There have already been a number of demonstration systems built, in two main areas:

1. As an intelligent interface between a user and an information repository where the user wants specific informa-

tion or non-specific information filtered out before it reaches them

1. In concurrent engineering where design-intelligent agents communicate with manufacturing-intelligent agents to ensure that the design can be manufactured

The group has also built a number of ontologies (models describing concepts) that are generic enough to be used to build particular ontologies that meet the requirements of an application domain.

Conclusions

The combination of object orientation, distribution, and semantic integration provide support for the component-based approach that will enable the creation of agile and perhaps even largely self-evolving style manufacturing systems of the future.

From this short discussion, it can be seen that there are a number of approaches to distributed component technology, and that there is plenty of support for the component and standard framework approach. However, at present, the requirements for semantic integration are only inherent in the NEWI and KIF/KQML technologies.

Ideally, future systems will comprise components based on a range of technologies—for instance, one could see an instance where there are NEWI, OpenDoc, and OLE integrated components that have been created based on an underlying ontological basis running over a CORBA platform that supports the defined KQML services.

References

[O'Call95] O'Callaghan, A., Overcoming the problems of OT adoption, *Object Expert Journal,* November 1995.

[Orfal] Orfali, Harkey, and Edwards, *The Essential Guide to Distributed Object Technology.*

[Cox87] Cox, B.J., *Object-Oriented Programming, an Evolutionary Approach,* Addison-Wesley, 1987.

[Chauv66] Chauvet, J.M., OT: Economics vs. technology, *Object Expert Journal,* Jan./Feb. 1996.

The following materials should also be consulted:

OMG/MFG/96-01-02, Manufacturing Enterprise Systems—A White paper.

OMG, The Common Object Request Broker: Architecture and Specification, Rev 2, July 1995.

MacBride, A. and Susser, J., *BYTE Guide to OpenDoc,* McGraw Hill.

Neches, R., et al. Enabling technology for knowledge sharing, *AI Magazine,* 12(3):36–56, Fall 1991.

Finin, T., et al., *Evaluation of KQML as an Agent Communication Language.*

Genesereth, M. et al, *Knowledge Intergchange Format v3 Reference Manual,* Computer Science Dept. Stanford University.

Uschold, M., Toward a methodology for building ontologies, *IJCAI-95.*

Labrou, Y. and Finin, T., A semantics approach for KQML—A general purpose communications language for software agents, *Proceedings of the 3rd International Conference on Knowledge and Information Management,* ACM Press, 1994.

Manufacturing Systems Integration (MSI) Research Institute, Loughborough University, Loughborough, Leicestershire LE11 3TU, England, Tel.: +44 1509 222919/228250, Fax: +44 1509 267725, Email: j.m.edwards@lboro.ac.uk

Designing and Documenting Componentware with Message Sequence Charts

Robert Nahm

In componentware, applications are built from software components. The main challenge is the integration of black-box components. The integration of components depends on the description of interfaces. An adequate interface description provides both a static and a dynamic view: the static view defines the signature of available operations; the dynamic view defines a protocol on how to use these operations. In CORBA (Common Object Request Broker Architecture), an IDL file (Interface Definition Language) describes the signature of operations, but a description of the protocol is missing. For this problem, a trace language like Message Sequence Charts (MSC) can help. MSC is a graphical language that describes traces of distributed systems. By means of traces, MSC diagrams describe how to use operations of components. In this way, MSCs describe the protocol of components. MSCs are perfectly suited to describe the interaction of components. This article gives an introduction to componentware, explains the working of componentware platforms, and discusses how MSCs help to improve the development process for componentware.

What Is Componentware?

Componentware transfers object-oriented principles to the world of applications. Componentware uses software components to build whole applications. Software-components are black-box implementations. Well-defined interfaces allow access to their functionality. Software-components together with their data are viewed as objects. Although processes or dynamic link libraries (DLL) can implement these objects, they behave as objects of an object-oriented program. They have properties like encapsulation and polymorphism and they communicate via method invocation.

In componentware, an application consists of and uses objects. This rule also applies to large, external components—for example databases or graphical user interfaces. Figure 1 compares two applications. The left application uses a traditional software development process, while the right application chooses the componentware approach. The large rectangles show the code that software engineers have to write; white ellipses within rectangles are local objects of an object-oriented program. The other ellipses show software components, and smaller rectangles present services that are not accessible by standard method invocation. Solid lines show object-oriented communication, like method invocation, and dashed lines show communication via customised APIs.

Componentware provides a series of advantages:

- Method invocation is the only communication mechanism of objects. A unified communication mechanism simplifies programming work.

- Objects communicate, although they are implemented in C++ or Smalltalk, or they run under UNIX or Windows. This allows communication in heterogeneous environments.

Traditional Software
Development

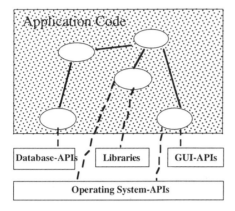

Software Development with
Componentware

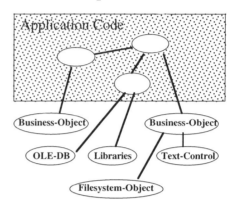

Figure 1. Comparison of traditional software development and software development with componentware.

- Objects communicate if they are located in the same process address space, on the same machine, or at different machines. Transparent distribution of objects simplifies the programming of distributed systems.

- Applications reuse the binary code of objects and not their source code. Reuse of binary code simplifies the compilation of applications and allows late binding of objects.

- The software engineers can use ready-to-use objects—for example, text control objects, spelling checkers, or databases. Reuse of commercial objects shortens the development process.

- The end user can configure the system at runtime. He can add additional components to a given application. For example, a compound document can integrate arbitrary editors and viewers at runtime.

Introduction to the Middleware Platform CORBA

Componentware platforms, for example, OLE or CORBA, enable the communication software of components. CORBA (Common Object Request Broker Architecture) is a middleware-platform standard of the Object Management Group (OMG). CORBA provides a language-, machine-, and location-transparent view of objects. But how does one implement a system in which, for example, a Smalltalk application running under Windows can call methods of a C++ software component running under UNIX?

The solution is to separate the interface of an object from the object itself. A separate document describes the interface of an object in a programming-language–neutral way. In CORBA, an IDL (Interface Definition Language) file specifies the signature of the object's interface. The signature describes the operations by their name, parameter, and result types. Data types, constants, and excep-

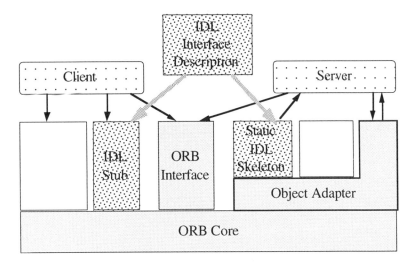

Figure 2. Common Object Request Broker Architecture (CORBA).

tions can be defined as well, and both client and server use this interface definition. The syntax of IDL is similar to C++. Figure 2 shows how the IDL description supports both client and server. The syntax of the client-side invocation is, of course, language-dependent. When invoking methods, there must be some module that transforms the language-dependant invocation into a language-independent format and vice versa. This is the responsibility of what is called a *proxy*.

The client needs a proxy to invoke the methods of a remote object. The proxy is a local object within the process address space of the client. In CORBA, the proxy is called an *IDL-stub*. The stub mimics the remote server. It transforms requests into language-independent interprocess communication. On the other side, the server has a proxy for all possible clients. In CORBA, this proxy is called an *IDL-skeleton*. The skeleton transforms interprocess communication (CORBA messages) into programming-language–dependant invocations. In CORBA, stubs and skeletons are

generated from the IDL description. Since proxies can be generated for different programming languages, CORBA enables the crossing of language and platform borders.

Besides the two proxies, the Common Object Request Broker Architecture (CORBA) itself consists of a number of modules. The following paragraph describes these modules and their responsibilities.

The Object Request Broker (ORB) is the core of CORBA. The ORB works like a software bus: It transports messages by using interprocess communication. Moreover, the ORB does administrative work—for example, it lists existing services. The ORB consists of the ORB core and the ORB interface. How to implement the ORB core is left to the platform provider, as long as it meets the standardised ORB interface. The Object Adapter (OA) controls the lifecycle of servers. It starts and terminates servers and causes loading and storing of object data. In addition, the OA transmits messages from the ORB to the IDL-skeleton.

What Is the Message-Sequence Chart?

The Message Sequence Chart (MSC) is a trace language that describe traces of distributed systems. MSC contains only a small set of language constructs. These are *instances, messages, tasks,* and *references.* Figure 3 presents an MSC diagram. Instances are vertical lines, which describe the behavior of objects. Each instance has an instance head, which carries the name of the object. On each instance, the time runs from top to bottom. The invocation of methods is described by messages. Messages are arrows between instances. Solid arrows present method requests. Text associated with an arrow contains the name of the method and the parameter list. Dashed arrows describe the passing of a result. Rectangles on single instances describe tasks that are performed by an object. Rectangles across several instances denote references to further MSCs.

For explaining the use of language constructs, Figure 3 presents a trace of the CORBA platform. The MSC diagram presents the scenario of a synchronous method invocation. Six modules take part in invoking a method:

the client with its IDL-stub, the server with its IDL-skeleton, the Object Request Broker, and the Object Adapter (see six instances within the MSC diagram).

In this scenario, the client and server are running on the same machine and the client is active. The server can be active or inactive. The client invokes the method by sending the request to its stub (see message "Request"). The IDL-stub transforms the language-dependent requests into a language-independent interprocess communication (see task "pack data"). It forwards the request to the Object Request Broker (see message "forward"), which in turn forwards the request to the Object Adapter.

The Object Adapter checks whether the server is available or active. If the server is inactive, then the Object Adapter activates it. A separate MSC describes the activation process (see MSC reference "find and activate server"). If the server is active, then the IDL skeleton receives the request. The skeleton transforms the language-dependent request into a language-dependent request format (see task "unpack data"). The IDL-skeleton invokes the request on the server.

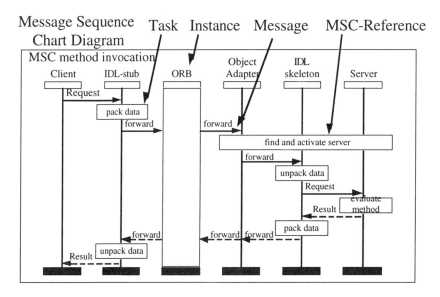

Figure 3. The invocation of a method in CORBA.

After evaluating the method (see task "evaluate method") the server directly sends the result back to the IDL-skeleton. The skeleton transforms the result into the language-independent format. The Object Adapter and the Object Request Broker forward the result to the IDL-stub. The stub transforms the result back to the language-dependent format of the client (see task "unpack data") and returns the result to the client (see message "Return").

Using Message Sequence Charts in the Development Process

Interfaces are necessary to encapsulate black-box implementations. They define a contract between a component user (client) and a component (server). An adequate interface description provides both a static and a dynamic view of the black-box implementation:

- The static view describes the signature of available operations. It describes the operation names, the parameter, and result types. In CORBA, an IDL file describes the signature of an interface.

- The dynamic view describes the protocol of the interface. The interface pro-

tocol describes in which order operations can be called. CORBA does not provide any formal mechanisms to describe such protocols. As we saw at the platform description, MSCs provide an ideal description to define traces of distributed systems. They explain in which order distributed objects exchange messages and perform tasks.

We suggest that MSCs be used for

- Designing the interaction of client and server objects

- Documenting the interface protocol of single components

Figure 4 provides an example how MSCs can describe the interaction of client and server objects. A client—for example, a Visual Basic Object—uses the service of a text editor and a spelling checker. The client implements the user interface, where the user inputs data. The data is checked for correct syntax and then it is stored by the text editor.

The MSC in Figure 4 presents this scenario. The client invokes the method "checkText" at the spelling checker. If the text has a correct

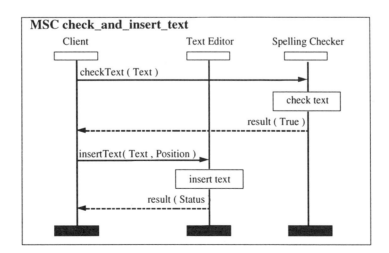

Figure 4. Designing client-server interaction with MSCs.

syntax [see "result(True)"], the client invokes the method "insertText" at the text editor. After the insertion, the text editor returns some status information of the operation. In this way large interactions can be described.

Figure 5 describes how MSCs can document the interface protocol of a single component. The MSC "insert_text" is extracted from the MSC in Figure 4. It presents the operations necessary to insert text in the text object. Of course, this is a very simple example. However, in many cases, a series of operations has to be executed to perform a certain functionality.

For a complete protocol description, a large set of MSC diagrams may be necessary. The language MSC provides a second type of diagram, called High-Level MSC (H-MSC), to structure the set of MSC diagrams. A High-Level MSC is organised as a graph. Conditions are the nodes of the graph. They present states of the component. MSC references are the edges of the graph. They refer to MSC diagrams that lead from one state to another state.

The H-MSC in Figure 5 presents the overall behavior of a text editor. There are two states of the text editor. The state "object is inactive" presents the state in which the text editor has not loaded the text object. The MSC "activate" leads from the state "object is inactive" to the state "object is active." The MSC "activate" de-

scribes the operations that are necessary to load the text object. If the object is active, then several scenarios are possible—for example, insert or delete text. For reaching the condition "object is inactive" the MSC "deactivate" will show the corresponding scenario.

Conclusion

One challenge of componentware is the integration of black-box components. A prerequisite for the integration is an adequate interface description. An interface describes both a static and a dynamic view. A static view describes the signature of available operations, for example operation names and parameter types.

A dynamic view describes the protocol in which order these operations can be executed. CORBA or OLE allows the description of the signature by formal languages like IDL or ODL. A formal description of the interface protocol, however, is missing. For this case Message Sequence Charts can bring a solution. MSC is a trace language that is perfectly suited to describe the interaction of objects and document the interface protocol of single components.

Robert Nahm is with Corporate Research and Development at Siemens AG.

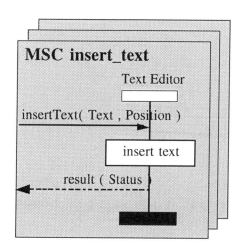
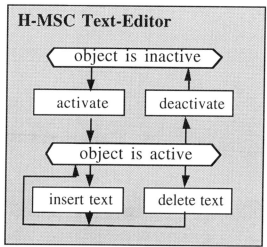

Figure 5. How MSCs can document the interface protocol of a single component.

Component Model for Managed Objects in Large-Scale Distributed Systems

Robert H. High, Jr.

Abstract

Object-oriented programming encourages programmers to think of their objects as highly independent and individualized. Conceptually, objects contain their own independent state and individual behavior. This notion does not scale well in large, distributed information systems. Commercial enterprises tend to have very large numbers of objects; often hundreds of millions of business objects. They also tend to have few administrators; perhaps only a few hundred. Thus managing the state and behavior of each independent and individual object quickly becomes impractical.

Procedural systems typically factor out large numbers by increasing the granularity of the object. Administrators do not normally manage individual records in a database; they manage an entire database table. The object, for all intents and purposes, is the table. The records are just data items within the object.

We propose alternatives for factoring out the complexity of scale. These mechanisms are based on aggregation techniques built on a component framework. Aggregates are collections of objects that can be used to factor common management policy. The aggregation approach is conceptually similar to the coarse-granularity technique used in procedural systems. However, it has the advantage of preserving the flexibility of independence and individuality that is available in object-oriented systems.

In this paper, we introduce a component framework for business objects. With that as a foundation, we then describe how components can he assembled along with object management mix-in classes to form a managed object. We discuss the effects of object granularity on object management. We demonstrate the use of aggregation in determining where objects are created, and in assigning objects names, security, and enterprise policy. Finally, we discuss some of the technical problems and solutions that are introduced by aggregation.

Problems in Large-Scale Distributed Systems

The prevailing issue of large-scale distributed systems is that of scalability and how to manage it. It is typical to find that an enterprise has hundreds of millions of objects. And very often, they have to manage these objects with perhaps only a couple hundred administrators. These administrators have the burden of ensuring that objects can be found, are accessed securely, are fulfilling the policies of the enterprise, and are maintaining the integrity of the enterprise data bases. And they have to be able to do so within the constraints of limited resources—they cannot, for example, afford to manage each individual object uniquely.

Notice that in the case that an enterprise has a hundred million objects and only a hundred administrators, each administrator is responsible on average for a million objects. Just the shear limitations of time prevent an administrator from being able to manage each of these objects individually.

We assume that it is well accepted that object-oriented programming is becoming increasingly important to the success of mission-critical applications—mostly for its ability to introduce abstract concepts that represent real-world business entities as well as laying the foundation for component re-use. Real-world abstractions enable better manipulation of information systems in matching them to the needs of the business. Component re-use enables enterprises to respond more affordably to business opportunities and requirements. These values are discussed at length in *Object Lessons; Lessons Learned in Object-Oriented Development Projects* [Love93], *Object-Oriented Technology: A Manager's Guide* [Taylo90], and of course *Object-Oriented Analysis and Design; With Applications* [Booch94].

Object-oriented systems also offer the opportunity to introduce concepts that can mask out the complexity of large-scale distributed systems. For instance, inheritance allows us to introduce administration for different services that achieve their differences not by introducing unique administration tools, but a family of tools that all derive and specialize a single, common administration model. In addition, polymorphism gives us the ability to apply the same administration tools to different infra-structure technologies—implementing the different mappings under the same interface framework.

Object-oriented programming introduces a down-side to large-scale distributed systems as well. That is, object-oriented programming emphasizes the notion of *encapsulation.* Encapsulation is the assertion that users of objects cannot and should not know how or depend on how the object is actually implemented [Wirfs90].

The desire to encapsulate is motivated by the impact that the lack of encapsulation in procedural systems had on programmers in main-taining their applications. When a user of a function comes to depend on the specific implementation of the function—for instance, on the structure of the data used within the function—then it becomes more difficult either to modify the implementation of the function or to move the user to a different but similar function as dictated by different business scenarios. In other words, re-use is significantly inhibited by the lack of encapsulation.

The characteristic of encapsulation in object systems suggests that objects are individual and independent—they contain individual state and independent behavior. Another way of thinking of this is that all objects are heterogeneous. This characteristic serves as a prime inhibitor to scalability. Heterogeneity demands that every object be administered individually. As we've already suggested, this creates unreasonably difficult logistical problems. Moreover, it prevents object-management systems from being able to factor out redundant information or optimize processes on common schemas.

To make this more clear, consider the problem of query. To find a particular record of interest in a procedural system, a relational database system will leverage the fact that all records in a given table have the same schema—they are homogenous. Further, it will organize data in the table around page-boundaries to maximize throughput—minimizing page faults—under the assumption that the entire table is co-located in the same storage space. This enables the database system to employ indexes and other sophisticated caching mechanisms to optimize the process of finding a particular record.

If, on the other hand, objects are independent, and moreover are distributed randomly across a distributed system, then building and maintaining indexes becomes a very difficult task. Complex two-phase protocols have to be used to assure the ACID (Atomicity, Consistency, Isolation, and Durability) properties of the index [Cerut93]. The overhead of keeping the index fully coherent in the absence of a shared memory space can even exceed the advantages that the index offers in performing searches across different objects.

Query just represents one problem of managing heterogeneous objects in a large-scale distributed system. A number of other scalability and management problems are inherent in large-scale systems as well. These include *naming, identity, security, lifecycle, persistence, externalization, transaction management, concurrence,* and *policy management,* etc.

A few of these problems are discussed further in the following sections. Throughout this paper, we discuss problems and solutions in the context of the CORBA distributed object programming model. CORBA is discussed in brief in the sidebar below.

Naming

End users must be able to find the objects they want to work with. One approach we've al-ready hinted at is to use a query mechanism—searching for an object whose attributes or instance data satisfy a given predicate (see the sidebar **Attributes and Instance Data**). Another approach to finding objects is to reference them by name. This suggests that objects should have human-readable names.

Care should be taken that the naming system does not introduce other management issues. For example, problems are created if the name space is flat. Doing so limits the usefulness of names. This is discussed below.

Since names need to be unique—if they're not then they don't do a very good job helping end users identify their objects—then in an environment with a hundred million objects you have to define a hundred million unique names. This in turn encourages the use of algorithms that compose names based on character permutations or other things that render the name cryptic and less meaningful to end-users.

To exemplify this better, it is important to understand some things about how names are used. First of all, names are by their very na-

---

CORBA

CORBA is the *Common Object Request Broker Architecture,* defined and published by the Object Management Group (OMG).

OMG is a consortium of more than 600 member companies representing both information systems industry vendors as well as customers. Their mission is to define standards relating to distributed object-oriented programming.

The CORBA standard defines the basic inter-workings and interoperability flows of an Object Request Broker

(ORB), that is, a broker of object requests. The standard is tailored for use between distributed objects. It includes specifications for how interfaces are specified using an Interface Definition Language (IDL), how the interfaces are made available at runtime, how objects are referenced and their implementations are activated, and also how memory is managed.

In addition, OMG defines a set of standards relating to object services, CORBAservices and CORBAfacilities.

These basically represent functions needed for managing objects in a distributed system. CORBAservices define general services such as Naming, Events, LifeCycle. CORBAfacilities define cross-domain and domain-specific facilities such as compound documents, internationalization, and systems management.

For more information about CORBA and the object services see the *CORBA, CORBAservices,* and *CORBAfacilities* books available from the OMG.

ture things that are significant to human beings—therefore, they should be things that humans can recognize. The best names are ones that convey meaning to the end-user. This helps them remember the name for future reference in getting back to the object of their interest. It also makes it easier to produce the name—the name should convey what the object means to the end-user.

Second, names are often the sole means by which identity is conveyed *between* humans. For instance, when a bank teller intends to operate on an account object, they will often identify that object not by anything they know intrinsically but rather by information that is conveyed to them by their customer—the person to whom the account belongs. Often in this case the customer will be given some piece of information, such as the account number, at the time the object is created with which to identify the object. The account number is in effect the name of the object.

Third, names are frequently relevant within a specific context. I might give an object the name "inspection-report." On its own, this name is relatively ambiguous. However, in the context of a real-estate transaction and more particularly the *Sale of the Kennison Estate,* this object obviously contains the results of the home inspection by the purchasing agent. This is well known because inspection reports are a common aspect of any real estate transaction.

Thus, names should be qualified—ideally they are hierarchical. Each level in the hierarchy creates a context which further qualifies the name and allows names to be conveyed unambiguously within their context. Further, partitioning the name-space, as in a name hierarchy, helps reduce name-collisions that might occur when the same name is used in different contexts. For instance, if one object is named with its account number and another object is named with its invoice number, and these two objects just so happen to both be named

"01-211470516," then they can be disambiguated by virtue of the difference in the context in which they are defined.

Security

Normally in business applications, objects contain important information. The value of this information has two implications: Objects shouldn't be available to anyone not authorized to have access to the information, and they shouldn't be changed by anyone not authorized to change it. In other words, access to managed objects should be controlled.

To control access to managed objects, a couple of other things need to be considered: To ensure that an end-user is prevented from performing unauthorized actions on an object, it is necessary to first determine who the end-user is (*authentication*). In addition, it is necessary to know what actions each end-user is allowed to perform on a given object (*authorization*). Each of these aspects is discussed further below. However, in addition to authentication and authorization, the topic of security usually covers the concerns of delegation, auditing, confidentiality and integrity, non-repudiation, and administration. These are important problems in large-scale distributed systems, but we do not discuss them further in this paper.

Authentication

The problem of authentication is particularly complex in distributed systems. It is not, however, a problem that is unique to object-oriented programming. Authentication addresses the problem of ascertaining who the end-user is, and then verifying that they are who they say they are—authentication is normally preceded by identification: requesting that users identify themselves and provide some sort of authentication information such as a password. Authentication, then, is the step of verifying the authentication information—usually by comparing it with previously known information about the user in a user database or *user-registry*.

The factors that make authentication complex in distributed systems are as follows: First, computing resources are by definition distributed—even all the way out to the client-user's office or desk-top. Client computers are inherently difficult if not impossible to secure. They are constantly at risk of being exposed to viruses and other malicious software; client-users themselves may be malicious and attempt to thwart their own computers via software or hardware; and they are physically exposed, so that others may attempt to attack vulnerabilities in the computer—even unbeknownst to the client-user/owner. Thus, client computers normally can not be trusted.

Second, server-side computers are often subject to similar kinds of risks—particularly if they are not physically protected in a traditional "glass house" computing center, or at least a locked closet.

Third, since authentication generally requires making comparisons to information in the user-registry, having too many user-registries can create administration problems and consequently additional security exposures. For instance, if a distributed system contains a user-registry on every computer that will serve objects to a client, then either the client-user needs to be known independently by each of those client-registries, or the client-user information needs to be replicated on each of the registries.

If the registries are independent, then failing to register the client-user to one or more of them could result in the user not being authenticated and therefore potentially being denied access to objects that they should have access to. On the other hand, if the registries have to be synchronized, then failing to update one of them could result in a client-user having access to objects that should be denied to them. For instance, if the user had legitimate access to an object and then leaves the company, and if a registry is not updated with the departure of the client-user, then it may continue to confirm the authenticity of the user and consequently allow access to the intended object.

Attributes and Instance Data

Typically we think of *attributes* as representing the instance of an object. Conceptually this is consistent with the way that attributes are used by client programs. We talk about an object having some number of attributes and infer that these can be acquired from or asigned to the object.

This, if course, raises a concern about encapsulation. If the instance data for an object is established as part of its interface, then it would seem we are giving client programs a prime opportunity to become dependent on something that is otherwise specific to the implementation of the object.

In fact, in CORBA, attributes are merely a convenient mechanism by which a special pair of methods can be defined in IDL. An attribute in IDL is a shorthand way of defining a get_* and set_* method—where the asterisk is replaced by the name of the attribute. By virtue of being methods, they can in fact be implemented in any fashion that is appropriate to the object. There may or may not be instance data in direct support of the attribute, and instance data can be kept without an associated attribute. Thus encapsulation is preserved.

We often refer to get_* and set_* as *attribute methods* to reinforce the idea that while specified as attributes for convenience, they are nonetheless methods at their core.

The authentication service should take into consideration these issues by avoiding any requirement that the client computer be trusted and by reducing the number of user registries that are needed across the distributed system.

Authorization

While authentication is fundamentally the same for both procedural and object-oriented programming environments, authorization is not. In procedural systems, the vast majority of access control is centered around data access. Thus access control is couched in terms of data access semantics—*read* and *write* and a few other variations such as *append*—leaving *execute* to cover the majority of all other cases. On the other hand, in object-oriented systems, the data is encapsulated behind object methods and thus the primary focus is on functional access semantics. Consequently, access semantics commonly supported by procedural systems are not applicable to object-oriented systems.

This issue is exacerbated by the number of different methods that can be defined to an object. Very often a business object may have 50, 100, or more methods. Each of these are of course introduced by business object programmers to perform vastly different functions. Access control semantics should have equal variety—for a trip-itinerary object some methods may be related to creating reservations, some may be related to verifying transportation schedules, and some may be related to establishing accommodation requirements. Each of these types of methods could have different access semantics—none of which are related to *read* or *write* semantics.

The access system must be flexible and extensible with respect to assigning access semantics to object methods. Business-object developers must have a means by which they control or at least influence the access semantics assigned to the methods they introduce.

Another major difference between procedural and object-oriented systems is the way that common access policies are assigned across a set of objects. As we've indicated previously, objects are aggregated within resource managers in procedural systems—in effect, objects are very course-grained. For instance, a database table is an *object* composed of data rows. This course-granularity serves a natural boundary on which access policies can be factored. A given user can be authorized to access a table, thus giving them access to any row in the table. The access policies do not have to be stored repeatedly for each row in the table. In systems with hundreds of millions of objects (data rows), this savings is substantial.

Similar aggregation boundaries do not exist naturally in distributed object systems. Objects are independent and individual. We need to introduce artificial aggregation boundaries to achieve the same factoring.

Lifecycle

Two major concerns surface in the area of object lifecycles: The first has to do with a separation of concerns—programmers often know *when* a new object should be created, but they don't necessarily know *where*. The other has to do with ensuring that the creation process considers all of the nuances of the situation in which the object will be used. Both of these concerns are discussed further.

New business objects are usually created in response to some action taken by an end-user. For instance, a new account object might be created as the result of a customer opening a new savings account. It is fairly straightforward to know when within the business logic the process of creating a new object should be initiated. However, in a large distributed system it is often not immediately apparent where that new object should be created. In fact, different enterprises may have vastly different policies on where new objects should be created. Or even within the same enterprise, the policy for where an object should be created may vary over time or depending on the type of object being created or the context in which it will be used.

To understand this better, consider the case of Tom Jennings. Tom has casualty and automobile insurance policies that he has purchased from the TopNotch Families Insurance company. One bright morning in the early spring while driving up highway 10 from Toronto to Owen Sound, Tom hit a patch of ice frozen in the cold of the night from the previous day's thaw. Tom lost control of his car, wiping out the front right fender of his car and tragically snapping off the tip of his right index finger.

TopNotch was on the scene almost immediately—second only to the wrecker service that is so well renowned in that part of Canada. (The emergency medical service arrived promptly after Tom's damaged car was hooked to the back of the tow truck.) Given the extent of the accident, two incident reports had to be filed for Tom—one covering the severed finger tip, and the other covering the damage to Tom's late-model car.

As it turns out, TopNotch Families has two processing centers, one handling automobiles and other personal property claims located in Sudbury and the other that handles medical and bereavement claims in Brantford. As a consequence of his mishap, three objects are created covering the totality of Tom's incident; a claim object representing the damages incurred to his auto, another claim object representing the damage incurred to his finger, and a case object that Tom's agent Darren, can use to follow the progress of Tom's claims.

These objects are created as a result of the incident. However, the auto claim object is created at the Sudbury processing center, the medical claim object is created at the Brantford processing center, and the case object is created at Darren's office in Toronto. The decision for

where each of these objects is created is based in part on the type of object and in part on the context in which the object will be used.

The lifecycle facility should be able to consider business conditions, scope, and locale as part of the object-creation process. It should be possible to initiate the creation process without having to be specific about where to create the object—allowing that to be determined elsewhere.

Policy Management

Enterprise policies are the prevailing stipulations that govern the way an enterprise conducts its business. Policies are derived from a number of sources and apply across a broad range of processes within the business. Government regulations may govern business practices and obligate the enterprise to certain financial and compensatory responsibilities—for instance, establishing sales or income taxes or regulating loan options. Market conditions may motivate certain product objectives—for instance, prioritizing the marketing of a more profitable product over others. Administration domains may establish operational conditions—for instance, limiting the use of printers to certain hours.

In an object-oriented system, policies usually constrain, condition, or annotate the behavior of objects to conform to a given enterprise policy. The separation of business logic from policy is a choice that the business-object developer must make. In general, policies change frequently—as often as business conditions change. The things that change often or between organizations should be separated from the things that remain relatively static over time. Policies are implemented as methods on a policy object—thus they can be arbitrarily complex. However, these can be implemented using simple programming approaches such as with script languages and rules engines. Likewise, most often policies merely establish thresholds that constrain business logic, boolean results that condition business logic, or side-effects that annotate business logic.

The process of applying policy to business in a large-scale distributed system is made problematic by three concerns: First, the application enterprise policy should always be current. Loan officers should be operating with the latest qualifying conditions when determining whether to present a loan product to a prospective applicant. The distributed nature of the system can increase the likelihood that a portion of the bank is operating with out-of-date loan qualification policies. Policies should be omnipresent in business logic, irrespective of the placement and execution of the object in the distributed system.

Second, business conditions change often, and enterprise policies change with them. It is important that policies are independent of the encoding of business logic—policy should not be hard-coded into business-application logic. It should be possible to update business policies without having to re-code, test, and certify mission-critical business applications. Just being able to avoid opening up the source code of business logic helps retain the integrity of the original code.

Third, policies are not usually uniform across all objects of the same type. For instance, an invoice may be subject to different tax rates depending on where the transaction is performed. Similarly, different stock-order objects may maintain different on-hand inventories depending on what season they are in. Thus, policies should not be applied on object-type boundaries.

Component Model for Business Objects

We introduce a component model for solving many of the problems that have been discussed here. The component model is simple and makes heavy use of OMG object services for managing business objects. These services are designed as frameworks. We assume an assembly model that enables collaboration between various programmers who have distinct roles and responsibilities that contribute to the overall system solution. The component model leverages aggregation as a technique for factoring common management information and tasks.

Frameworks Are Important

Undoubtedly, each of the problems that we've identified in this paper relating to object management in large-scale distributed systems have numerous solutions. The solutions that we recommend are defined as *frameworks*. Frameworks are important because they define the protocols between collaborating objects and thus they enable the federation of different object implementations within the system.

Ted Lewis, et al define a framework as "an object-oriented class hierarchy plus a built-in model which defines how the objects derived from the hierarchy interact with one another" [Lewis95]. Nearly any solution to the problems we've identified will necessarily involve collaboration between multiple service objects. In addition, the nature of object-oriented systems encourages collaboration between business objects. This collaboration must be well formed.

Moreover, different implementations of the same service objects will often lend different qualities of service. In a large-scale system, there is normally a requirement for a variety of qualities of service, depending on the applications in use in different parts of the enterprise. This drives the need for different implementations of service objects. In addition, the same type of business object may be implemented differently in different parts of the same enterprise.

However, to ensure holistic integration across the enterprise, it is important that different object implementations interact with each other—indifferent to the disparity in their implementation. The framework serves as a judiciary for governing the federation of different implementations.

Component Assembly

The component assembly model for business objects assumes a separation of roles. These roles include *system providers, object providers, application assemblers,* and *application and system administrators.* Of course the net result is made available to *end-users.*

This separation of roles recognizes that components are developed by ISVs (Independent Software Vendors) for use in many different institutions, and each institution may exploit the component for slightly different purposes. Thus, object components are produced by *object providers.*

Subsequently, institutions that acquire these components will have to customize them to their particular institution's needs. This is performed by *application assemblers.*

The object provider must have some set of assumptions they can make about the operational environment in which they will run—they create a dependency on a particular system environment that is supplied by a *system provider.*

Once a set of business objects have been customized, they are ready to be deployed and administered by *application administrators.* Setting up the system with the platform dependencies and distinguished runtime (nonbusiness) objects is the responsibility of *system administrators.*

This separation of roles allows the right skills to be applied at each phase of the object lifecycle. Object providers supply business objects based on their domain knowledge. System providers supply services based on their expertise in distributed system technology issues. Application assemblers bring these two together based on their knowledge of information systems and topology in use at their enterprise. Application and system administrators control the operation of application objects and services based on their knowledge of enterprise and system policy.

The Component Model

To help manage objects in a distributed system, we introduce a simple component model for business objects. This model is based on the exploitation of system frameworks. The component model assumes that business objects are created independently and without consideration for the system parameters in which they will be executed. Thus business objects are created by object providers.

The model then assumes that service behavior is attributed to business objects for the sake of managing the object in the form of service-specific base classes. For instance, to make a business object secure, you would inherit a security base class. This is performed by the application assembler as a customization step before deploying the object in their enterprise.

We make use of the object services defined by OMG and the respective base class for each of those services. For each service, the corresponding service-specific base class is as follows:

Naming. None is required other than that the object be served with a persistent reference (see the sidebar **Persistence of Object References**)

Identity. CosObjectIdentity::IdentifiableObject

LifeCycle. CosLifeCycle::LifeCycleObject

Events. CosEventComm::PushConsumer, CosEventComm::PullConsumer, CosEventComm::PushSupplier, or CosEventComm::PullSupplier

Persistence. CosPersistencePO::PO

Externalization. CosStream::Streamable
Transactions. CosTransactions::Transactional-
Object
Concurrency. CosConcurrencyControl::
LockSet
Security. somSecure::Securible[1]
Policy. PolicyRegions::PolicyDrivenBase[2]

Making a business object manageable is mostly
a matter of deciding what types of management are needed for the object, and then mix-
ing-in the base-class for the respective type of
management. For instance, if you had created
a business object for a car rental form and decided that rental form objects need to be persistent, transactional, and secure, then you
should mix-in the implementation class[3] for
CosPersistencePO::PO, CosTransactions:: Transac-
tionalObject, and somSecure::Securable.

To name an object requires only that the
managed object have a persistent reference—
no mix-in class is needed to manage the object
with a name.

Object Management Based on Aggregation

A key to solving the scalability concerns of object systems is the use of aggregation. Trygve
Reenskaug, et al define three types of aggregation: *encapsulation, embedded,* and *virtual*
[Reens96]. Embedded aggregation is where
sub-objects are aggregated by reference—sub-
objects continue to be visible and addressable

---

1. OMG does not define a base class for secure objects. **som-Secure::Securable** is introduced by SOMobjects.
2. Policy management is a recently adopted CORBAfacility originating from X/Open. It is introduced here with its X/Open Common Management Facilities interface name.
3. Som ORB vendors may provide the implementation for each of the object services, including the mix-in base classes, in a different implementation subclass.
  This is the case with SOMobjects—for instance, **somPersistencePO::PO** is the implementation class for **CosPersistencePO::PO**.

outside of the aggregate. We make heavy use of
embedded aggregation in each of the scenarios
described below.

Aggregation allows us to factor common
information, policies, and roles across a large
number of individual objects. Aggregates can
contain heterogenous or homogenous object
types—they are only homogenous with respect to a particular administrative perspective. Thus, an administrator can effectively ad-
minister a large number of objects by merely
administering the aggregate.

Naming Contexts

The Naming service provides the ability to
bind a managed object with a human-readable
name. That name can later be used to resolve
back to the bound object.

The naming service introduces *naming-
contexts* that contain name bindings. Since
naming contexts are themselves managed objects, they can be bound in to other naming
contexts to form a name tree (actually a graph).
An example name graph is depicted in Figure 1.
In this diagram, B and **C** are naming contexts
bound in the *root* naming context, F is a naming context bound in B, and **H** and **I** are naming contexts bound in C. All the others are objects of various types bound in their respective
naming contexts.

AR names are relative (to the naming context in which their object is bound), but a compound name can be formed to traverse through
the name space. For instance, /B/F/M is a compound name from the root naming context
that traverses through naming contexts B and F
to the object M. Although not depicted in this
figure, objects can be bound multiple times in
the same naming context with different names,
or in different naming contexts with the same
or different names.

The advantage of a naming context is that
it aggregates a large number of objects at a single point in the name space—all objects in the

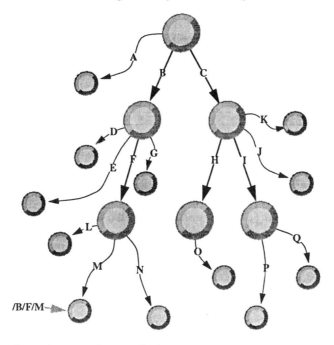

Figure 1. Object naming based on naming contexts.

same naming context have the same name path. More importantly, it sub-sets the namespace— reducing the number of names the application has to deal with for a set of related objects.

This characteristic, along with the fact that the same object can be bound in multiple naming contexts, can be exploited by applications. They can create containers of related objects that have some common relevance to an end-user. The application can then iterate over all of the objects in the container based on their common relevance to the user.

For instance, Darren could create a new context for Tom's car accident. In it he could bind all of the witnesses to the incident including other motorists, the tow-truck driver, and the emergency medical services team. He could then ask his application to send out a form letter to each of them asking for their view on whether Tom was driving too fast for the weather conditions. He could have created additional naming contexts for similar purposes covering other incidents—maybe even involving some of the same people (highway 10 is a dangerous stretch of road in the early spring).

Security Object Groups

Authorization is used to ensure the client user is allowed to access the target object with the requested method—the target object in this case is known as a *secure object*. Secure objects are aggregated into *security object groups* as depicted in Figure 2. Access controls are assigned to each secure object group which identify the *rights* a given user has to any object in the group. In addition, each method in a class is ascribed *required-access-rights*—the rights a client user must have in order to invoke that method. Thus, the rights granted to a user to access an object, by virtue of that object being within a particular object group, are compared with the required-access-rights for that method. If they match, then access is granted. Otherwise, the method request is rejected.

Security object groups serve to factor common access policies across a large set of objects. This reduces the amount of storage that has to be allocated for maintaining access policies, and reduces administrative burden—the administrator only has to update access policies on the security object group, knowing that those policies will apply to all objects within that security group.

Security object groups can contain heterogenous object types—the differences in access semantics for different methods in different classes is handled with required-access-rights labels associated with each secure method.

In the example depicted in Figure 2, Joe has the access rights of a *bank-teller*. This enables him to access the deposit method. It also enables him to access the get_balance and withdraw methods as well.

Notice that Jordan has the *customer* access right. This would enable her to access the get_balance method on the objects in the security object group. Presumably an of the objects in this security object group belong to her—perhaps each of these are accounts that she has at this bank. She probably would not have been granted the *customer* access right to objects in another security object group not belonging to her. In other words, access rights are not necessarily shared across different security object groups—they are unique to each security object group.

Factories and Factory Finders

A factory is any object that is capable of creating another object. A factory introduces one or more constructor methods that encapsulate the specifics of creating a particular object based on its type or the context in which it will be used. In many cases, the constructor method will present a business semantic—for instance, the open_new_account method may be used to create new *Account* objects. A client can initiate the creation of an object by locating an appropriate factory and invoking its constructor method.

The factory finder serves as a front-end to the factory service—a distinguished naming context in which all factories are bound. Factories are bound in the factory-service–naming context with a set of properties that define, for

---

Persistence of Object References

CORBA defines an object reference as a pseudo object that can be used in a program to refer to an object. References are distributed by the CORBA object request broker (ORB), but are produced and managed by the object adapter (OA).

The reference contains room for information that is supplied by the object adapter: *reference data.* The reference data is immutable and is carried around in the reference. The object adaptor can use the reference data to help it identify the object that it refers to. Object adapters typically do this by embedding an object key in the reference data. Typically, the object adapter will produce a key at the time the object is created or the first time the object is exported from a process. Later, when the reference is used, the object adapter uses the key to map back to the target object.

Effectively, a reference is persistent only to the extent that the mapping between the key and the target object is persistent. If the object itself is transient, then the mapping will only be valid for the period that the object exists in memory— the reference is only persistent if the object can be reproduced in memory.

If the object is persistent, then there will usually also be a piece of information that is needed to retrieve the object's persistent state—the *data key,* for instance. This information or some mapping to it can serve as the object key. Since the object key can be related to the data key, the original object can be recreated, even if it was removed from memory. The mapping between the object reference and the object can be preserved, thus rendering the reference persistent.

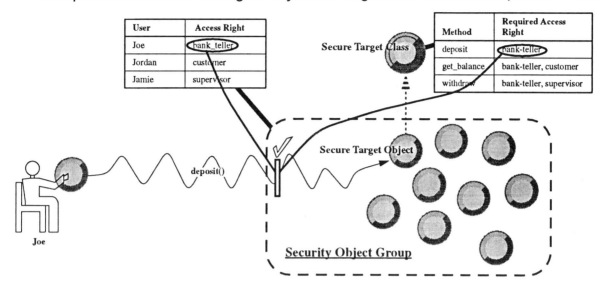

Figure 2. Access control based on secure object groups.

instance, the kind of object(s) they create, the conditions under which they create them, and the circumstances under which they are applicable. A factory can be found by searching over the factory-service–naming context for a factory whose properties satisfy the needs of the client.

The factory finder creates an indirection to the factory service. This indirection allows application assemblers to provide additional control over how factories are found—based on location, types, load, or other factors that may be unique to a given institution. This is depicted in Figure 3. Application assemblers can control factory finding in two ways: by controlling how the factory-service predicate is formed, and by filtering the factories returned from the factory service.

Factories help make the object system more scalable by factoring the details of instance construction over a large number of objects the factory knows how to create. Likewise, the factory finder helps isolate the client program from the unique aspects of where to create objects under what conditions, making them more portable to different enterprise scenarios. The institution can control the object-

creation process by participating in the factory-selection process.

Policy Regions

The policy management service provides a mechanism with which to constrain, condition, or annotate the behavior of managed objects in accordance with enterprise policy. Managed objects are registered with a policy region. Policy objects are assigned to the policy region for each type of object in the region. Policy objects support methods that when invoked by the managed object, can constrain, condition, or annotate the system or business logic. This is depicted in Figure 4.

Often an enterprise will have multiple policy scopes that apply to different aspects of their business. These scopes may represent different geopolitical, regulatory, divisional, or administrative boundaries. In addition, an enterprise may have multiple policy domains that represent different interests within their business. For instance, a policy scope could be all objects that are subject to a given taxing authority. And a policy domain could be those activities that relate to legislative constraints. A policy region represents a policy scope and/or

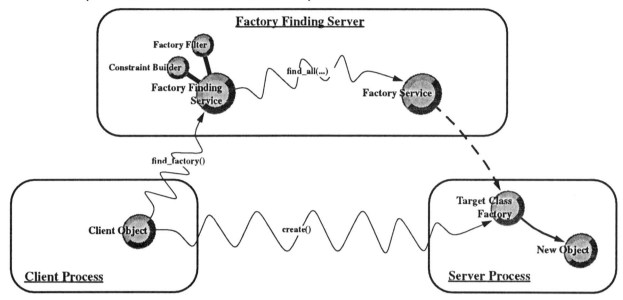

Figure 3. Object Creation Based on Factory Finding.

domain. In many cases, it is necessary for a given managed object to be a member of multiple policy regions to properly represent all of the policy influences that affect it.

The managed object obtains one or more policy objects from its policy regions. Thus, different managed object instances of the same type can be subjected to different policies depending on how an enterprise is organized. Changing the policy for a given managed object is a simple matter of moving it between policy regions. Likewise, changing the policy for an entire policy scope or domain is a matter of changing the policy object(s) associated with a policy region.

The managed object provider must define the semantics of the policy object methods; however, the application assembler provides the implementation of policy objects—the policy object should implement the policies of its institution for a given policy scope or domain. In addition, the application assembler is responsible for parameterizing their factories to ensure objects are created in the right policy region.

There are two types of policy objects. *Policy validation objects* are used during the normal operation of the managed object to ensure

the object behaves and maintains state in conformance with the enterprise policy. *Policy initialization objects* are used during the creation of the managed object to ensure it is created and initialized in conformance with the enterprise policy.

Policy regions factor common enterprise policy over a large set of objects. This reduces the number of places where policy has to be defined, which in turn reduces the opportunity for policy to be out of date. By separating the policy logic into policy objects (independent of the business object), these can be updated without having to re-certify the business object. Finally, the policy region enables the policy for an individual object to be changed by merely changing the policy region to which it belongs.

Effects of Object Granularity

The granularity of an object will have an effect on the level of manageability that needs to be applied to an object, as well as the level of manageability that can be afforded by an object. Before discussing this further, we should point

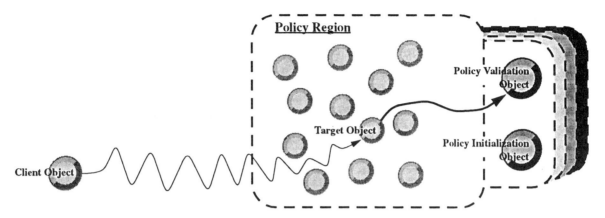

Figure 4: Enforcing Enterprise Policy through Policy Regions.

out that object granularity can be measured in a number of ways: in terms of the number of bytes of instance state contained within the object, the number of methods it supports, the number of classes that are composed in its hierarchy, the lines of code contributing to the object's implementation, or even more esoteric metrics such as the relevance of the object concept to end users.

The measurements that you use will change where your object ends up on the granularity scale, but it doesn't necessarily change the issues and solutions that should be considered in your object design. The granularity of an object can be classified in the following categories: *Designed, Reusable, Shared, Distributed, Managed,* and *Conglomerate.* Each category is progressive—including the characteristics and concerns of its preceding (less granular) counterparts. The categories are discussed below:

Designed: At one extreme, very fine grained objects typically represent primitive or constructed data types with mathematical operations. These kinds of objects typically have a negligible effect on computing resources and

require little or no management other than object creation and destruction. This is normally handled easily within the application and almost always is used within the same language in which it is implemented.

We refer to these object as *designed* to infer that someone decided that the function was worth implementing using object-oriented programming—they are *objects by design.* Otherwise, designed objects merely represent the entry into the object-granularity spectrum.

Reusable: If the class of an object is re-used as part of different but similar concepts, typically it will have to support being initialized in different ways. For instance, if an object is developed to support the concept of a bank customer, then maybe it only has to be initialized with the customer's mailing address and social security number. If the class of that object is reused to develop the concept of a bank customer that is also an employee of the bank, then maybe that type of object has be initialized with the employee-customer's home address, social security number, *and* employee identification. The object will support different initializers for each of the situations in which it is used.

Often, the additional initializers are introduced in sub-classes that specialize the original object for use in the new situation.

Shared: An object whose classes are shared introduces a number of special object model problems. To begin with, sharing an object class implies that a given object will consist of classes produced in different places from different sources. This disparity could be as close as sharing between two tightly collaborating programmers in the same department, or as far apart as two completely independent vendors producing object components purchased and combined by the programming shop at a large institution, or any combination in between.

The farther apart the source parties, the more complex the sharing gets. First, the various parties may use different programming languages—C or C++ in one case, OO-COBOL or even Java in another case. This suggests that a language-neutral binary packaging technology is needed in the object model. It also suggests that interfaces should be specified in a neutral language such as CORBA IDL.

Second, if an object component is purchased from an independent vendor, very often it will be available only as a binary—without source code. This leads to the problem that if the component ever had to be replaced—due to bug fixes or just general improvements in the code—it should be possible to do so without having to recompile the sub-classes. We refer to this as *release-to-release binary compatibility* and it should be supported in the object model.

Third, encapsulation is always an important aspect of object-oriented programming. It is even more essential to enable object sharing. If implementation specifics are allowed to seep out, then sharing the object or replacing the original implementation without effecting the objects or classes that depend on it gets much more difficult.

Distributed: To use an object from two or more vastly disparate applications often requires being able to access the object from other processes or even other computers. The object is in effect distributed. It must be possible to communicate the object or a reference to the object. Likewise, it must be possible to invoke methods on the object remotely. The CORBA object request broker architecture serves this purpose.

To help locate the object from remote clients, it is useful to associate the object with a server process. The server to which the object belongs helps establish the identity of the object.

Local/remote-transparency becomes an important issue for distributed objects—actually, for the clients of distributed objects. Having to know whether an object is local vs. remote reduces the flexibility that the application assembler has to place objects in the distributed system where they make the most sense. For instance, for one enterprise, having an account object close to the production databases may make sense, whereas for another enterprise, having that same account object close to the platform-officer to whom the object belongs may make more sense. If the knowledge of an object's location has to be embedded in any clients that use it, then that makes the clients more intolerant to the object being placed elsewhere.

Similarly, having to establish location information for an object to communicate with it simply distracts the business object developer from performing their primary task—that is, producing business function.

A key element to providing local/remote transparency is being able to make it appear to the client that invoking a method on an object is always the same. In other words, in the case that the object is remote, a proxy should be injected in the local environment that masquerades as the target, remote object. Method requests on the object are always invoked as methods on a local object, irrespective of whether the target object is local or remote.

By the time an object is course-grained enough to afford being distributed, it is probably large enough to be recognized by an end user.

Managed: Soon after an object is distributed and recognizable by an end-user, issues of object management start to arise. Many of these issues have been the topic of this paper. They include naming the object, being able to distinguish between two object instances, controlling access to the object, and the process of creating an instance to ensure it is located in the most appropriate place. It also includes ensuring that objects conform to enterprise policy and maintaining their instance state persistently and with integrity. In addition, it also means systems managing them including identifying, tracking and resolving problems and tuning their performance, and administering them within the object system.

The issues that surface with managed object design are scalability and robustness, and separation of responsibilities in their construction and deployment.

Conglomerate: Very large-grained objects represent the other extreme in objects. We refer to these as conglomerate objects. Naming contexts and collections are good examples of these types of objects. They contain so much state data that often it is difficult to maintain them entirely within memory. Certainly they cannot be handled easily as monoliths—moving them between processes and machines, for instance, requires transferring massive amounts of data.

These types of objects tend to violate many of the assumptions that go into the design of object services for managing objects. For instance, they usually require a more incremental persistence model. Likewise, move and copy lifecycle operations need to be handled differently to avoid overloading streams, etc.

The granularity spectrum is depicted in Figure 5. As with all classification schemes there can be lots of exceptions. The intent of the classification scheme isn't to be definitive as much as it is to put design discussions in perspective. We often observe that differences in opinion on design points can be distilled down to a difference in assumptions about object granularity. We recommend that every object design should start with a declaration of the object granularity to which the design applies.

Technical Problems and Solutions

The use of aggregation—particularly embedded aggregation—introduces some additional problems of its own. Specifically, objects belong to the aggregate only by reference. They continue to be accessible directly, without the involvement of the aggregate. Thus the aggregate cannot be used to guarantee the enforcement of policy obligations. They can only be used as a convenience for factoring administrative policy. It is still up to the underlying object system or diligent administrative practice to guarantee that policy obligations have been met.

Another issue related to the fact that objects can be accessed independently is that they can also be destroyed unbeknownst to the aggregate. Object management aggregates often represent residual metastate relating to the objects contained in the aggregate. At the very least, the aggregate generally contains a reference to the object. In other cases, such as naming contexts, the aggregate also includes discrete information about the object like names and other properties. Consequently, aggregates introduce potential garbage collection issues—including the aggregate itself in the case that all of its members are destroyed.

Granularity	Classification	Characteristics	Concerns
Very Fine Grained	Designed	Objects created/used within component Relevant only to program	Minimize conceptual resources
Fine/Small Grained	Reusable	Increased reusability—initialization can be contextual to reflect current needs	Instantiator must recognize special requirements of object class
Medium Grained	Shared	Class sharing across language/ programmer boundaries Possible relevance on screen or as data access objects	IDL—language neutral class specification Release-to-release binary compatibility Class sharing Encapsulation essential
Large/Coarse Grained	Distributed	Associated with server process Relevant between applications Recognizable by end-user	Local/remote transparency Distributed lifecycle Object Refs/Proxies to Objects
Very Large Grained	Managed	Named Identifiable Secure LifeCycle Policy Driven Persistent and Transactional Systems Managed Relevant to Administrator	Scalability/Robustness Separation of Programmer Responsibility from Administrative Duty
	Conglomerate	Lots of state-data Naming contexts Collections	Incremental Persistence Model

Figure 5. Effects of object granularity.

Many of the garbage collection problems introduced by aggregates can be solved merely by ensuring the destructor methods of a managed object properly un-register the object from its respective aggregates. This can be achieved by supplying this behavior in the mix-in classes for the respective object service.

However, in some cases, the object services do not provide a mix-in class in which this behavior can contribute to the managed object— such as the case with Naming. In other cases, even if the behavior can be supplied, the managed object may not even be aware of what aggregates it has actually been assigned to. And in yet other cases, it may not be able to afford the expense of cleaning up in the main-line code path along with destroying the object. In these cases, more traditional garbage collection mechanisms should be used.

Finally, since aggregates are typically implemented as objects themselves, they too need to be managed. When the aggregates are managed using the object-management techniques we've described here, then service interdependencies are formed that cause object management to become relatively monolithic—that is, employing any amount of object management with a given business object results in many, if not all, other aspects of object management getting loaded at runtime as well. This may not be a problem, per se, other than that it increases the footprint of the runtime, but it does suggest that object-management designs should be optimized for the presence of all other services rather than optimized to optional co-dependence on other services.

Summary

Large scale systems are burdened with the implications of large numbers of objects and few administrators for managing them. Object designs must include provisions that enable business objects to be managed in an efficient manner. Management systems need to introduce artificial boundaries on which management information and policies can be factored. Doing so reduces the amount of resource that redundant management information consumes, and reduces the amount of management policy that has be created and maintained by administrators.

Likewise, providing support for management behavior is a distraction for business-object developers—it takes them outside of their main area of expertise and responsibilities. Making use of a component model that allows business objects to use pre-defined and implemented management behavior is essential. Not only does it free business-object developers to concentrate on their main task at hand, but also enables domain experts in the area of information systems infrastructure to ensure the rigor and completeness of management services.

Finally, it is important to recognize the effects of object granularity on scalability. Object granularity should be considered in object design and used to motivate an appropriate level of management. Small-grained objects can often forego any significant object management. Large-grained objects have significant relevance to end-users and require substantial management. Very-large-grained objects require vastly different object-management philosophies.

We make heavy use of aggregation techniques—particularly, embedded aggregation— for instituting management boundaries on which administrative policies can be factored. We also recommend the use of a component model that assumes the use of OMG object services mix-in classes for attributing management behavior to business objects. While the use of aggregation introduces certain additional problems, we believe the benefits of aggregation far out-weigh their burden.

Glossary

ACID (Atomicity, Consistency, Isolation, and Durability): ACID properties are a minimum characteristic of a transaction service. Atomicity, isolation, and durability lead to consistency of data.

business object: An object containing business methods; logic and state—intended for use within business applications. Typically, business objects are managed objects.

CORBA (Common Object Request Broker Architecture): CORBA is a specification for a standard object request broker defined by the Object Management Group (OMG).

embedded aggregation: A form of aggregation in which the sub-objects remain visible from outside the aggregate.

enterprise policy: Conditions, constraints, or obligations (in the form of annotations) that govern the behavior of business (or system) objects.

IDL (Interface Definition Language): IDL is part of the CORBA specification for defining *interfaces* and *operations.* In SOMobjects, *interface* is synonymous with *class,* and *operation* is synonymous with *method.*

ISV (Independent Software Vendor): A company that independently produces software for commercial use.

managed object: An object managed by one or more object services.

object: "Of a technology relating to any product with the word 'object' in its title; widely believed to be capable of speeding development as each deadline is exceeded; according REUSABILITY a higher priority than USABILITY." [Kelly95]

OMG (Object Management Group): The OMG is a consortium of over 600 member companies whose mission is to create specification standards for distributed object-oriented systems.

SOMobjects: The IBM product that implements CORBA and other OMG-related standards.

References

[Booch94] Booch, G., *Object-Oriented Analysis and Design With Applications*, Benjamin/Cummings Publishing, Redwood City, CA, 1994, *ISBN 0-8053-5340-2.*

[Cerut93] Cerutti, D. and Pierson, D., *Distributed Computing Environments,* McGraw-Hill, New York, 1993, ISBN 0-07-010516-2.

[CORBA95] *CORBA: The Common Object Request Broker: Architecture and Specification,* July 1995, Object Management Group, Inc.

[COSS95] *CORBAservices: Common Object Services Specification,* March 31, 1995, OMG Document Number 95-3-31, Object Management Group, Inc.

[FAC95] *CORBAfacilities: Common Facilities,* mid-1995, Object Management Group, Inc.

[Kelly95] Kelly-Bootle, S., *The Computer Contradictionary,* MIT Press, Cambridge, MA, 1995, ISBN 0-262-11202-7.

[Lewis95] Lewis, T., et al., *Object Oriented Application Frameworks,* Manning, Greenwich, 1995, ISBN 1-884777-06-6.

[Love93] Love, T., *Object Lessons: Lessons Learned in Object-Oriented Development Projects,* New York, 1993, ISBN 0-9627477-3-4.

[Taylo90] Taylor, D.A., *Object-Oriented Technology, A Manager's Guide,* Addison-Wesley, Reading, MA, 1990, ISBN 0-201-56358-4.

[Reens96] Reenskaug, T., Wold, P., and Lehne, O.A., *Working With Objects, The OOram Software Engineering Method,* Manning, Greenwich, 1996, ISBN 1-884777-10-4.

[Wirfs90]Wirfs-Brock, R., Wilkerson, B., and Wiener, L., *Designing Object-Oriented Software,* Prentice Hall, New Jersey, 1990, ISBN 0-13-629825-7.

Trademarks

OMG® is a registered trademark of the Object Management Group, Inc.

CORBA, CORIBAfacilities, and **CORBAservices** are trademarks of the Object Management Group, Inc.

X/Open is a trademark of X/Open Company Ltd

IBM is a registered trademark of International Business Machines, Corp.

SoMobjects and **System Object Model** are trademarks of International Business Machines, Corp.

What Is a Pattern?

Frank Buschmann and Peter Sommerlad

Patterns have been drawing considerable attention over recent years: conference papers [Coad92], workshops, tutorials, forums for electronic discussion, and whole books [Gamma95], [Coad95], [Copli95] are devoted to patterns. The pattern community even started its own conference series, the PLoP (Pattern Languages of Programming). A European complement of this conference—EuroPLoP—will be held in Germany next year. With all this enthusiastic discussion, it is as if patterns were the climax of the "object wave."

But after all, what is so exciting about patterns? Is it just the buzzword of the 90s? Is the software community try to sell an old technology under a new name? Will patterns be offered, like stolen watches, by shady figures standing at dark corners? Or is there something underlying the notion of patterns that in fact justifies the recent hymns? The goal of this paper is to explore what patterns really are.

To understand patterns it will be helpful to discuss the ideas underlying this new discipline in software engineering.

When experts work on a particular problem, it is unusual for them to tackle it by inventing a new solution completely distinct from existing ones. They often recall a similar problem they have already solved and reuse the essence of its solution to solve the new problem. This kind of "expert behavior," the thinking in problem-solution pairs, is common to many different domains, such as building architecture [Alexa79], economics [Etzio64], and software engineering [Beck94]. It is a natural way of coping with any kind of problem or social interaction [Newel72]. You

see, patterns are nothing new. We find them everywhere and use them every day.

We also find many patterns in software architecture [Copli92], [Gamma95], [Coad95], [Copli95]. Experts in software engineering know these patterns from practical experience and they follow them in developing applications with specific properties. They use them to solve design problems both effectively and elegantly.

A pattern for software architecture describes a particular recurring design problem that arises in specific design contexts and presents a well-proven generic scheme for its solution. The solution scheme is specified by describing its constituent components, their responsibilities and relationships, as well as the ways they collaborate.

Example
Observer [Gamma95]

Context
A component uses data or information provided by another component.

Problem
Changing the internal state of a component may introduce inconsistencies in co-operating components. To restore consistency we need a mechanism to exchange data or state information between them. Associated with this problem are two forces:

- The components should be loosely coupled: the information provider should not depend on details of its collaborators.

- The components that depend on the information provider are not known *a priori*.

Solution

Implement a change propagation mechanism between the information provider—the subject—and the components dependent on it—the observers. Observers can dynamically register or unregister with this mechanism. Whenever the subject changes its state, it starts the change propagation mechanism to restore consistency with all registered observers. The changes are propagated by invoking a special update function common to all observers. To implement the change propagation—namely, the passing of data and state information from the subject to the observers—you may either use a pull-model, a push-model, or a combination of both.

But after all, what are patterns good for? You can distinguish three fundamental properties:

Patterns document existing, well-proven, design experience. They are not invented or created artificially. Rather, they "distill and provide a means to reuse the design knowledge gained by experienced practitioners" [Gamma93]. Those familiar with an adequate set of patterns "can apply them immediately to design problems without having to rediscover them" [Gamma93]. Previously, this knowledge existed only in the heads of a few experts. Patterns make it more generally available. You can use this expert knowledge to design high quality software for a specific task.

Patterns are a means for documenting software architectures. They can describe the vision you have in mind when designing a software system. This helps others to avoid violating this vision when extending and mod-

ifying the original architecture or when changing code.

Patterns provide a common vocabulary and understanding for design principles [Gamma93]. Pattern names, if chosen carefully, become part of a widespread design language: they facilitate an effective discussion of design problems and their solutions. There is no need to explain a solution to a particular problem with a lengthy and complicated description. Instead, you use a pattern name and explain which parts of a solution correspond to which components of the pattern or to which relationships between them.

You see, there is nothing special about patterns. They deal with the many small and also the bigger problems software developers encounter every day. Every pattern also helps to solve only one problem and does this independent of other patterns. Patterns do not claim to solve all problems, or the software crisis as a whole. For many important areas in software development, such as security, transactions, or fault tolerance, ether no or only few patterns are available.

Furthermore, patterns do not define a process model for software engineering or outdate existing ones. Finally, patterns do not provide a new method for software development. Patterns complement existing techniques and methods in a very pragmatic way. They provide solutions for very specific design problems, problems which cannot be addressed by methods and process models, or by object technology in general.

On the one hand, this may sound pretty disillusioned. On the other hand, if you think about it, you will realize the great potential embedded in this pragmatism. Patterns do not praise new, yet unproven wisdom, but are based on existing experience in building high quality software. They describe what worked in the past, not what might work in the future. Patterns make this precious knowledge available for you, ready to use, and without the need to gain years of experience on your own. This is the big strength of patterns and you should build on this strength only if you talk about the impact and promises of this discipline. Otherwise, as with artificial intelligence, you my raise overdrawn expectations that patterns cannot fulfill and which finally let patterns fail.

References

[Alexa79] Alexander, C., *The Timeless Way of Building,* Oxford University Press, 1979.

[Beck94] Beck, K. and Johnson, R., Patterns Generate Architectures, *Proceedings of ECOOP'94,* 139–149.

[Coad92] Coad, P., Object-Oriented Patterns, *Communications of the ACM,* 33(9), 1992.

[Coad95] Coad, P. with North, D. and Mayfield, M., *Object Models—Patterns, Strategies, & Applications,* Yourdon Press, Prentice Hall, 1995.

[Copli92]Coplien, J. O., *Advanced C++—Programming Styles and Idioms,* Addison-Wesley, 1992.

[Copli95] Coplien, J.O. and Schmidt, D.C., Eds., *Pattern Languages of Program Design,* Addison-Wesley, 1995 (reviewed *Proceedings of the First International Conference on Pattern Languages of Programming,* Monticello, Illinois, 1994).

[Etzio64] Etzioni, A., *Modern Organizations,* Prentice Hall, 1964.

[Gamma93] Gamma, E., Helm, R., Johnson, R., and Vlissides, J., Design patterns: Abstraction and reuse of object-oriented design, *Proceedings of ECOOP'93,* 406–431.

[Gamma95] Gamma, E., Helm, R., Johnson, R., and Vlissides, J., *Design Patterns—Elements of Reusable Object-Oriented Software,* Addison-Wesley, 1995.

[Newel72] Newell, A. and Simon, H.A., *Human Problem Solving,* Prentice Hall, 1972.

Frank Buschmann is software engineer at Siemens AG, Corporate Research and Development, Munich, Germany. He has experiences in building bussiness applications and industrial automation systems. Currently, he is responsible for the research activities in software architecture and patterns. With colleages he is writing a book about patterns which is due early next year. Frank.Buschmann@zfe.siemens.de

Peter Sommerlad is a software engineer and researcher at Siemens AG, Corporate Research and Development, Munich, Germany. He has been working on object-oriented software engineering tools and innovative approaches to software development incorporating frameworks. He is investigating the application of design patterns for domain-specific framework construction.

Why Objects Are Not Enough

Cuno Pfister and Clemens Szyperski

Abstract

Object-oriented programming hasn't created a
viable software component industry. From a
technical perspective, the reason for this failure
lies in an insufficient consideration of the
unique requirements of component software.
Object-oriented programming too often con-
centrates on individual objects, instead of
whole collections of objects—i.e. components.
Component-oriented programming requires
more stringent information hiding, a more dynamic approach, and better safety properties
than object-oriented programming does.

Introduction

The existence of a software crisis had been
recognized as early as 1968 [Naur69]. It became clear that to overcome this crisis, software construction would need to be treated
as a genuine engineering discipline. In a mature engineering discipline, new products
are rarely developed from scratch. Instead,
products are composed out of readily available components. It has become obvious that
a true software-component market is necessary in order to overcome the software crisis.
Yet even today it is rarely possible for an
end-user to buy some necessary new functionality in the form of a new software component, and integrate it into his or her software environment.

Proponents of object-oriented programming have often promised that objects will create a component market [Cox90]. However,
the opposite has happened [Niers91]. While it
was still possible to call procedural libraries
compiled with one compiler from a program
compiled with another compiler, this is not
possible anymore for class libraries. Suspi-
ciously, the standards that have been proposed
in order to overcome this deficiency [Lau94,
Brock95] don't require the use of object-oriented languages at all. The most successful
component market so far, a niche market created by Microsoft's Visual Basic [Visua92], involves no object-oriented programming language either.

Has object-oriented programming failed,
as stated in [Udell94]? Or is it just a matter of
time until it catches on and delivers on its
promises?

In this article it will be argued that object-
oriented programming as it is usually defined
is too narrow a concept. Focusing on individual objects is misleading and often results in
software that cannot be used as components.
In the following sections, several aspects of
component software will be discussed, some of
which shed light on the relation between components and objects.

A component is defined as a collection of
cooperating objects, with a clearly defined
boundary to other objects or components.
Objects inside of a component typically are in-
tertwined tightly, while interaction across the
component boundary is relatively weak.

In this article, wherever the intention is
clear, the terms *object* and *class* are used inter-
changeably.

Decomposition—Aspects of Granularity

In this section we investigate a number of different aspects that ask for decomposition of programs into units of varying size and coherence, e.g., into classes or modules. In each case the governing rules of decomposition are different. In particular, it is important to understand the implications of the granularity of a particular decomposition.

Units of Abstraction

From a software architect's point of view, the hardest design problem is how objects should interact. In order to keep complexity under control, it is desirable to isolate objects as much as possible. On the other hand, if complex interactions can be handled by a library, the complexity for the library's clients may be reduced considerably. Libraries that define interactions for objects are called frameworks [Deuts89]. The main benefit of a framework is the design expertise embodied in it, ready for reuse by less skilled programmers. Objects in a framework are tightly coupled, with a much weaker coupling between frameworks. A framework may completely hide its implementation, and only provide an abstract interface to the outside. Such a so-called black-box framework [Johns94] acts as a unit of abstraction. Its classes are rarely meaningful if considered individually.

Units of Analysis

Any system of at least medium size needs to be hierarchically decomposed into smaller units, and the coupling between those units should be as weak as possible. Only a good decomposition allows one to reliably construct (synthesize) or understand (analyze) a complex system. Examples where analysis of system parts are required are: verification according to a specification, testing, type checking, version control, etc. In fact, all phases of a software life cycle ask for one sort of analysis or the other.

The coupling between units determines the extent to which any form of analysis of one unit needs to take properties of other units into account. In an unstructured system where all units are tightly entangled with all other units, separate analysis of units is hopeless and a global analysis must be undertaken.

Decomposing a system into bounded units of analysis is necessary in practice when a system becomes too large for a global analysis to be feasible. Even more important, decomposition into bounded units of analysis is necessary in principle when a system is meant to be independently extensible [Szype96]: since components in such systems are added by the client on demand, there is no meaningful systems integration phase that the software engineer can rely on, and therefore global analysis cannot take place before it is too late.

Some forms of global analysis are unavoidable. A typical example is the final version check when integrating a component on demand. However, those "last minute" checks should only flag problems that are meaningful to the user, such as the correctable problem of a version mismatch.

Where possible, it is advisable to aim for the smallest units of analysis possible. In some cases, such as local type checking, individual objects or even individual methods can form units of analysis. Quite often, the units need to be larger and encompass interacting groups of objects bound by a certain contract, modules, or whole subsystems.

Units of Compilation

Incremental compilation can speed up the edit–compile–link–run cycle considerably. Increments can be applications, modules, classes, or statements. In a component software world, complete applications don't exist anymore;

thus the application as unit of compilation is not relevant anymore.

Units of compilation relate to the units of analysis discussed above. A tradeoff faced when dealing with compilation units of finer granularity, e.g., classes, is the small extent of the compiler's context. In particular, tight interactions with auxiliary constructs outside the class, but within a "natural" module enclosing the class, may require combined analysis. This can be simplified when compiling at the level of modules. For even larger units, compilation speed becomes an issue. Given a fast compiler, e.g., [Wirth92], both modules and classes appear as reasonable units of compilation [Szype92]. Translating individual statements is only practical in interpreted languages.

Units of Distribution

Today, applications, and sometimes components, are the typical units of distribution. Individual objects are rarely worth the administrative effort and cost of distribution.

In a system where objects are the only structuring facility, it becomes very difficult to extract and package a suitable subset of objects, in order to ship them as a component. In practice, it becomes almost impossible to extract meaningful collections of objects out of an unstructured collection that consists of thousands of objects. What is needed is a static higher-order structuring facility, such as a module construct [Wirth82]. Even modules may prove insufficient, and constructs such as systems [Carde89] or libraries [Apple92] may have to be introduced for more complex components.

Units of Loading

After the installation of a component, it may be loaded on demand. In fact, in a networked environment the component might not even be locally installed. Instead, the component is fetched from a remote site when needed

[Arnol96]. However it is done, a dynamic linking facility (DLLs) must be available. If a language is designed to support dynamic linking, it is sometimes called a dynamic language [Apple92]. Since objects in a component typically interact closely, loading one object would immediately cause the loading of the other objects. It is usually more efficient to load the whole component as a unit.

Loading a new component into an already running system requires that the version of the new component be checked first. Loading must be prevented if the new component uses other components that are not available in this environment, or that have an incompatible version. Incompatibility due to incorrect versions is called the syntactic fragile base class problem. For maximum compatibility, version checking should occur per object, rather than per component [Creli94].

When objects of different origins are loaded, name collisions may occur. There must be a mechanism to prevent such collisions. The safest way is to define a hierarchical naming scheme, where the top-level names are registered with a global naming authority as with Oberon/F [Obero96] or Java.

Microsoft's Component Object Model [Brock95] is interesting in that it uses 128-bit numbers, so-called GUIDs (globally unique identifiers) to prevent name collisions. These numbers are constructed out of a machine location and the time when the number was created. COM is noteworthy also in that it does not allow one to change an existing interface. Instead, a new interface must be added to a component.

On the level of programming languages, the loading of new objects must not invalidate other already loaded objects merely by the fact of loading. This rules out the use of languages whose type systems require global analysis for type checking, e.g., as in Eiffel [Meyer92, Szype96].

Units of Dispute

If a system composed of several components fails, component vendors tend to blame each other for the problem. To minimize this undesired effect, it is vital that errors remain contained in individual components. This means that they should be clearly attributable to their particular component, and they should not endanger the system as a whole (bug containment). The most severe nonlocal errors are violations of memory integrity, i.e., dangling pointers and memory leaks. To solve this problem on the level of programming languages, completely typesafe languages are required. With current language technology, this in turn mandates the use of garbage collection. Examples of typed garbage-collected languages are Oberon [Reise92], Sather [Szype94], and Java.

In technical terms, safety means that invariants can be guaranteed. Information hiding on the level of objects allows one to guarantee invariants over the hidden instance variables. For example, whenever the width of a rectangle is changed, the method which changes the width can also update an instance variable that contains the rectangle's area. In this way, the invariant *area equals width times height* can be maintained. Safety can be increased if more global invariants [Holla92] can be specified and enforced by a closed unit. This is possible if information hiding is done at the level of components, rather than at the level of individual objects.

Safety features of a language either prevent errors, or allow one to exactly pinpoint the component where an error occurred. In a system composed of independently developed components, this helps clients to find out which vendor's software has failed. If a component's identity (boundary) could not be clearly determined, it would become too difficult to find out which vendor was the culprit.

Units of Remoting

Component-integration standards such as SOM/DSOM and COM/Network OLE provide facilities to remote objects over a network to remote machines. As a consequence, method calls are not local procedure calls anymore, but incur remote procedure calls that are several orders of magnitude slower than local procedure calls. This makes it important to keep tightly coupled objects together on the same machine. This is another example where components should be treated as basic units, rather than individual objects.

Units of Extension

A component may not provide completely new functionality, but may instead extend existing functionality or implement existing interfaces. Typically, several objects of a component must be extended simultaneously. The coupling between the objects forming an extension is tighter than between extending and extended components.

For example, the file abstraction of an object-oriented operating system may define separate abstractions for files and for file-access paths. A concrete implementation of the file object would contain information about the disk sectors occupied by the file, while the access-path objects would contain their current position and hidden information, such as the disk sector of the current position. To implement these objects in an efficient and safe manner, it is necessary that the implementation of the access path object has direct access to the implementation of the file object. However, access to either implementation from outside of the component must be prevented.

The lack of a visibility scope which can enclose several objects is a fundamental weakness of most object-oriented programming languages. Notable exceptions are modular languages such as Modula-3 [Nelso91] and Oberon.

The designers of C++ [Ellis94] acknowledge the problem by allowing private parts of a class to be selectively exposed to certain explicitly named *friends*. While perfectly general, this approach is entirely unstructured. The namespaces currently proposed for C++ are mere units of name space management.

Java's packages are more flexible than C++ namespaces, but still don't allow one to solve the problem outlined above, i.e., it is not possible to export two Java classes that allow mutual access to their implementation details, while hiding them from clients.

A unit of analysis must not be broken up into several units of extension. Otherwise, an extension could be integrated into a target system with incomplete context, i.e., not with the same context as at the time of analysis. For example, if a particular object is not as general as its interface seems to indicate, and therefore this object can only function in certain constrained contexts, then it is normally not wise to sell this object as an individual product.

Units of Maintenance

Software products are rarely perfect upon release. Usually it is necessary to distribute updates which correct errors, which are more efficient, or which add new features. If an update changes the inner workings of the component, depending client components may break, because they relied on a particular behavior of the objects from which they inherited. This is called the semantic fragile base class problem.

For traditional procedural libraries, this problem is addressed by procedure update systems, e.g., [Fried91]. While not solving all problems and putting a significant burden on the updating programmer, these systems allow clients of procedural libraries to be migrated, even at run-time, to an updated version of a library without forcing a rewrite of the clients.

Unfortunately, with today's specification techniques it is not possible to specify the internal self-recursion patterns of a class, short of publishing the complete source code (white-box frameworks). The cause of the problem is the overly tight coupling of base class and extending class via inheritance ("inheritance breaks encapsulation"). Since it is not desirable to use the source code of a component as its specification (which would freeze the component once and for all), a looser coupling via composition instead of inheritance is preferable.

A Shift of Focus

The discussion of various aspects of a component's life cycle has shown that many important issues do not become apparent if only individual objects are considered. A more global point of view is required. The focus shift from objects to components has subtle, but far-reaching implications. It is claimed that the narrow object-centric perspective is the main culprit that has prevented object-orientation from realizing its full potential, i.e. from creating a viable component software industry. To name the required focus shift, the following definition is given:

A programming language is called component-oriented if it provides polymorphism, information hiding over several objects, late binding and late linking, and type safety [Szype95].

The requirement to support late binding and late linking is sometimes attributed to so-called "dynamic" languages.

This is in contrast to the typical interpretation of object-oriented programming [Wegne87], which consists of polymorphism, information hiding over individual objects, late binding only, and inheritance (or delegation).

Note that the definition of component-orientation does not emphasize inheritance (or delegation) as a key ingredient, but it does emphasize polymorphism. This reflects the belief that current code inheritance (and delegation) mechanisms are not sufficiently controllable (or even understood!) when used to couple code across components. Of course, a programmer may choose to use the full object-oriented programming spectrum within a component.

It cannot be excluded that with the development of more restricted forms of inheritance or delegation, and in conjunction with improvements of interface definition techniques, the direct reuse of code across components may become justifiable in the future.

Standards

SOM is a binary object integration standard that supports typical OOP features such as multiple inheritance and metaclasses. COM, on the other hand, is a binary component integration standard. COM strictly separates interfaces from implementations, but supports neither subclassing (inheritance) nor subtyping.

Proponents of both standards claim that they solve the fragile base class problem. In reality, both SOM and COM solve the syntactic fragile base class problem, but only COM addresses the semantic fragile base class problem, by relying on composition for code reuse, rather than inheritance. This observation will serve as a typical example of misunderstandings caused by not distinguishing between object-oriented programming and component-oriented programming.

COM defines a reference counting scheme for memory management. In principle, this allows one to implement automatic garbage collection, as proven by [Obero96]. However, reference counting is usually done manually, and is thus the primary source of errors when doing OLE programming. Furthermore, reference counting fails for cyclic data structures. The cy-cle-breaking rules of COM are unnecessarily complex. SOM has no provisions for automatic memory management. Reference counting is defined only for some OpenDoc-specific SOM classes. Automatic garbage collection for SOM does not seem possible.

Conclusions

While object-orientation has received much attention in recent years, this attention has been too narrowly focused on individual objects, and on objects that don't need to be distributed in binary form. In a component software market, objects don't come alone; and they come without source code. When components, i.e., whole collections of objects, must be distributed and integrated, new problems arise that are usually ignored, e.g., the inherent conflict between inheritance and information hiding, or the need for information hiding on units larger than objects.

These issues are not academic; they are well known to some of the vendors who are attempting to create a software component industry. It is important that developers also become aware of these issues before trying to coerce traditional OOP techniques to construct component software solutions.

References

[Arnol96] Arnold, K. and Gosling, J., *The Java Programming Language,* Addison-Wesley, 1996.

[Apple92] *Dylan—An Object-Oriented Dynamic Language,* Apple Computer Eastern Research and Technology, Cambridge, Massachusetts, 1992.

[Brock95] Brockschmidt, K., *Inside OLE 2nd Ed.,* Microsoft Press, 1995.

[Carde89] Cardelli, L., *Typeful Programming Technical Report Nr. 45,* DEC Systems Research Center, 1989.

[Cox 90] Cox, B. J., Planning the Software Industrial Revolution, *IEEE Software,* 7(6), November 1990.

[Creli94] Crelier, R., *Separate Compilation and Module Extension Dissertation No 10650,* Swiss Federal Institute of Technology, Zurich.

[Deuts89] Deutsch, P., Design Reuse and Frameworks in the Smalltalk-80 System, in Biggerstaff, T.J. and Perlis, A.J., Eds., *Software Reusability,* Vol. 2, ACM Press, 1989.

[Ellis94] Ellis, A. and Stroustrup, B., *The Annotated C++ Reference Manual,* Addison-Wesley, 1990 (corrected reprint 1994).

[Fried91] Frieder, O. and Segal, M.E., On dynamically updating a computer program: From concept to prototype, *Journal on Systems Software,* 14, Elsevier, 111–128, 1991.

[Holla92] Holland, I.A., Specifying Reusable Components Using Contracts, *Proceedings ECOOP '92,* Lehrmann Madsen, O., Ed., *Lecture Notes in Computer Science, Nr. 615,* Springer-Verlag, 1992.

[Johns94] Johnson, R., *How to Design Frameworks Tutorial Notes of Object-Technology at Work,* University of Zurich, 1994.

[Lau94] Lau, C., *Object-Oriented Programming Using SOM and DSOM,* Van Nostrand Reinhold, 1994.

[Meyer92] Meyer, B., *Eiffel—The Language,* Prentice Hall, 1992.

[Naur69] Naur, P., and Randell, B., Eds., *NATO Conference on Software Engineering,* Garmisch, Germany, October, 1968 NATO Science Committee, Brussels, 1969.

[Nelson91] Nelson, G., Ed., *Systems Programming with Modula-3,* Prentice Hall, 1991.

[Nierstrasz 91] Nierstrasz, O., *The Next 700 Concurrent Object-Oriented Languages—Reflections on the Future of Object-Based Concurrency Object Composition,* Tsichritzis, D., Ed., Centre Universitaire d'Informatique, University of Geneva, 1991.

[Obero96] Oberon microsystems, *Oberon/F User's Guide,* 1994.

[Reise92] Reiser, M., Wirth, N., *Programming in Oberon,* Addison-Wesley, New York, 1992.

[Szype94] Szyperski, C., Omohundro, S., and Murer, S., Engineering a programming language—The type and class system of Sather, *Proceedings, First International Conference on Programming Languages and System Architecture, Lecture Notes in Computer Science, Nr. 782,* Springer, 1994.

[Szype92] Szyperski, C., Import is not inheritance—Why we need both modules and classes, *Proceedings ECOOP '92,* Lehrmann Madsen, O., Ed., *Lecture Notes in Computer Science, Nr. 615,* Springer-Verlag, 1992.

[Szype95] Szyperski, C., *Component-Oriented Programming: A Refined Variation on Object-Oriented Programming,* The Oberon Tribune, Oberon Microsystems, Inc. Zurich, December 1995.

[Szype96] Szyperski, C., Independently extensible systems—Software engineering potential and challenges, *Proceedings, 19th Australasian Computer Science Conference Australian Computer Science Communications,* 18:1, 203–212, January 1996.

[Udell94] Udell, J., ComponentWare, *BYTE,* 19(5), 46–56, May 1994.

[Visua92] Visual Basic Microsoft, Seattle, 1992.

[Wegne87] Wegner, P., Dimensions of object-based language design, *Proceedings, Second Conference on Object-Oriented Programming Systems, Languages, and Applications (OOPSLA'87) Special Issue of SIGPLAN Notices,* 22(12), 168–182, October 1987.

[Wirth92] Wirth, N., Gutknecht, J., *Project Oberon—The Design of an Operating System and Compiler,* Addison-Wesley, New York.

[Wirth82] Wirth, N., *Programming in Modula-2,* Springer, New York, 1982.

Dr. Cuno Pfister is with Oberon Microsystems, Inc., Technoparkstrasse 1 CH-8005, Zürich, Switzerland. Phone: (+411) 445 1751. Fax: (+411) 445 1752. Email: pfister@oberon.ch.

Associate Prof. Dr. Clemens Szyperski is Director, Programming Languages and Systems, Research School of Computing Science, Queensland University of Technology, Brisbane Q 4001, Australia. Phone: (+617) 3864 2132. Fax: (+617) 3864 1801. Email: c.szyperski@qut.edu.au

Oberon/F: A Cross-Platform Component-Oriented Framework

Cuno Pfister and Clemens Szyperski

Abstract

A software component is a collection of objects that can be loaded dynamically. It constitutes a black-box with respect to the object implementations that it contains. A framework that defines abstractions that can be implemented as components, and that consists of components itself, is called a component framework. Oberon/F is a component framework that runs on multiple platforms. Its compound document architecture hides much of the complexity and the differences between OLE and OpenDoc, and thus makes components easier to implement and makes them independent of a particular component standard or graphical user interface.

Introduction

The software industry currently forces an unpleasant choice upon its customers: a customer either buys off-the-shelf standard software, or embarks on the hazardous and expensive adventure of building the desired solution from scratch. There are hardly any intermediate approaches between *make* and *buy*. The ever increasing complexity of today's software forces more and more customers to favor standard software, even where it is only marginally suitable for the particular business processes.

This state of affairs cannot continue for long; it does not address the customers' real needs, and the accelerating complexity of current software development is becoming increasingly unmanageable. As has happened before in every mature engineering discipline, this dilemma will be solved by introducing standard components from different vendors that can be mixed and matched with custom components, in a customer-specific assembly.

Today we can observe the beginning of such a transformation in the software industry. A component software industry can only develop on a large scale if there are suitable integration standards. Earlier lower-level integration standards, such as Unix pipes, have turned out to be too restrictive and inefficient to serve as basis for advanced graphical applications. But with Microsoft's COM/OLE [Brock95] and the Component Integration Lab's SOM/OpenDoc [Lau94, OpenD96], the first practical standards are now in place.

Still largely missing is experience in the design of component-based solutions, and the tools and methodologies that support component production, documentation, and assembly. To some degree, traditional object-oriented tools and methods can be used when dealing with the objects contained in a component, but the relation between objects and components, and between components themselves, is less well understood and supported.

Component Framework

Frameworks are class libraries that define interactions between their classes [Deuts89]. They are natural candidates to support component software. They already imply a more architecture-centric view of software compared to the object-centric view that is still so common today. Basically, a framework embodies an abstract design for a family of related problems; it is a problem-specific "design method" cast in software. A framework that provides a strong decoupling between itself and its extensions is called a black-box framework [Johns94]. In particular, it hides implementation details of the objects that it contains, and it can be used without its source code. This matches well the nature of components, which are black-boxes themselves. The following definition assumes a component being defined as a dynamically loadable black-box consisting of a collection of interacting objects:

A framework that defines abstractions that can be implemented as components, and that consists of components itself, is called a component framework.

Component frameworks shift the emphasis away from individual objects on the one hand and away from entire monolithic applications (application frameworks) on the other. Most current framework efforts, e.g., Apple's OpenDoc Development Framework ODF [ODF96], are intermediate steps between traditional application frameworks such as MacApp [MacAp96] and true component frameworks. They basically treat components as mini-applications, and emphasize internal implementation aspects over external component interface aspects.

Goals

The development of the component framework Oberon/F was started in late 1992. The first release came out in late 1995; recently the third release became available [OM96]. Oberon/F is a horizontal framework for industry-standard operating systems and graphical user interfaces. Currently, there are versions for Windows 3.1/95/NT and Mac OS. It

serves as a basis for vertical third-party frameworks, e.g., in the real estate business. Current applications include numerical algorithms and data visualization, database front-ends, data acquisition for chemical reactors, training, etc. When designing the framework, the following goals were pursued:

- *Platform Independence.* Programming interfaces are completely portable across the supported platforms. Yet the correct look-and-feel of the underlying platform is supported. This is achieved by defining suitable abstractions, which hide the peculiarities of user interface details such as menus or windows. Binary data files, including documents, are portable as well.

- *Safety.* A solution consisting of interacting components is only as reliable as its weakest component. Ideally, an arbitrarily bug-ridden component should not be able to bring down the application as a whole. This is important in a component software world, since components may come from places where there are no quality guarantees, e.g., from the Internet. Some minimal guarantees can be achieved by using typesafe programming languages with garbage collection, such as Java [GJS96] or Oberon [RW92].

- *Power and Simplicity.* Oberon/F is based on Oberon, which combines the power of "real" languages such as C++ with the simplicity of "scripting" languages such as Basic. Similarly, the framework is positioned between simple but limited 4GL environments such as Visual Basic [VB92], and flexible but complex environments such as Taligent's Common-Point [Cotte95].

- *One Language.* Oberon is used for component creation (real programming) and for component assembly (scripting). This eliminates the scalability problems that arise inevitably when working with a separate scripting language.

- *Efficiency.* The complete framework, including text and form subsystems, the integrated development environment, on-line documentation, etc., is fully implemented in Oberon, and is lean enough to be shipped on only two floppy disks. The compiler produces fast machine code; no interpretation is involved.

- *Compound Document Architecture.* Document parts are powerful user interfaces for software components. Integrating components translates to composing documents. Oberon/F, including the development subsystem, is fully based on a document-centric programming model. Global resources such as windows or menus are hidden behind more abstract and uniform concepts. For example, a part does not need to behave in a special way just to be able to function as a root part of a document.

- *OLE and OpenDoc Compatibility.* The differences between OLE and OpenDoc are hidden by a general container abstraction. The user interface, e.g., for the activation and selection of document parts, automatically conforms to OLE guidelines under Windows, and to OpenDoc guidelines under Mac OS.

- *Resources as Documents.* Resources such as menu definitions, string translations, or dialog boxes are stored as editable compound documents. In particular, user interfaces are not compiled into source code. Dialog boxes can be used while they are being edited; there is no need for special preview tools.

- *Maintainability.* For best maintainability and as mentioned above, Oberon/F is completely written in the component-oriented language Oberon. Component-orientation is related to object-orientation, but puts more stringent demands on information hiding, on dynamic loading, and on safety, while relying less on inheritance.

Design

Architecture

Oberon/F consists of three layers. The bottom layer is a module library that defines basic services such as file I/O, a package of mathematical functions, access to run-time type information (Meta), etc. The library services are relatively independent from each other, i.e., they are not frameworks.

The middle layer is the core framework. It provides Oberon/F's compound document architecture, which is a hierarchical version of the MVC scheme [Krasn88]. Graphics, persistent objects, an extensible file conversion mechanism, an OLE- and OpenDoc-conformant container abstraction, and support for user interaction via controls and other GUI elements are defined in the core framework.

In the top layer, several application subsystems are provided. They are extensions of the core framework, and some of them are extensible frameworks of their own. The Text subsystem is a simple word processing framework, while the Form subsystem provides a dialog box layout editor framework. Both texts and forms are containers, i.e., they allow the embedding of arbitrary Oberon/F views (or OLE / OpenDoc parts). Typically, a component is either one single tool module, or an entire subsystem. Oberon/F abstractions are represented graphically as follows:

A rectangle with a thin outline denotes an Oberon module; a rectangle with a thick outline denotes a whole subsystem, i.e., a collection of related modules.

Dynamic Loading of Modules

Modules are Oberon's information hiding units. A module may contain an arbitrary number of item definitions (constants, types, variables, procedures, classes). Some of the items may be exported, i.e., may be accessible from other modules. Other items may be kept hidden, as are other implementation details such as the implementation of a procedure or method. Modules are light-weight dynamic link libraries (DLLs), i.e., a module is loaded as a whole when it is needed. If it is not needed during a session, it is not loaded and does not consume main memory. A module that is loaded remains loaded, unless it is explicitly unloaded (terminate and stay resident). When a module is loaded, a version check is performed to guarantee that all imported items are available and have the correct version. This version check is performed on a per-object basis, i.e., only the items actually used are being checked. Later releases of a module may add new items without invalidating clients, i.e., the module loader implements a light-weight object model in the sense of COM or SOM. This solves the syntactic fragile base class problem. A module's exported procedures, so-called commands, may be activated directly by the user, by their names. This allows one to conveniently develop and test new modules independent-

ly of whether there already is a suitable graphical user interface or not. User interface issues thus can be largely decoupled from software engineering issues.

Distribution of Components

When independently developed modules are combined, name clashes may occur. This name space pollution problem is one of the typical problems associated with component software. A global registration service could solve this problem by checking registered module names for uniqueness.

In order to reduce the number of necessary registrations, a two-level scheme is used for Oberon/F. It is possible to register a unique module name prefix, e.g., Text. This prefix is shared by a whole number of related modules. Then the owner of the prefix may locally assign unique suffixes to the modules. For example, there are modules TextModels, TextViews, and TextControllers. Such a collection of related modules is called a subsystem. Typically, the distribution package of a software component consists of one tool module, e.g., a spelling check module, or of all modules of a subsystem. Installation and deinstallation of a subsystem is simple: a subsystem is stored in its own subdirectory. Installation thus means copying the subdirectory; deinstallation means deleting the subdirectory. For the purpose of distribution and remote updating, Oberon/F comes with a tool that allows one to package several files together into an ASCII file, which can be transferred via the common electronic mail systems.

Development Environment

The development environment consists of a fast native-code compiler, a symbolic debugger, browsing tools, etc. All these tools consist of Oberon modules, which constitute the Dev subsystem. Thus the development environment is not separate from the framework, but is one of its applications! The compiler is incremental, with single modules as compilation units. Type checking across module boundaries is performed, i.e., the correct use of imported items is checked at compilation time. Compilation is very fast: the complete system, from kernel to compiler, compiles itself in less than three minutes on a medium 486 machine. The symbolic debugger displays objects in hypertext form. Pointers can be followed by clicking on hyperlinks. The debugger uses the standard text subsystem for this purpose. In other words, the debugger is also part of the Dev subsystem, i.e., it is an application of the framework itself.

Black-Box Design

Oberon/F is a black-box framework, i.e., it comes without source code. This is possible because in order to achieve code reuse, the framework relies more on composition than on inheritance. This leads to more explicit and better specified component interfaces, rather than the blurred contracts induced by inheritance [Willi94].

Public abstractions in Oberon/F are mostly abstract, i.e., cannot be instantiated directly. Instead, concrete implementations can be obtained via directory objects, a concept similar to factory objects. Concrete implementations are not exported, and thus cannot be extended via inheritance. Most Oberon/F services are replaceable, e.g., it would be possible to replace the text subsystem at run-time with an extended implementation, without invalidating any existing client software, such as the compiler or debugger.

Safety

Components should be less tightly integrated than objects, but they are necessarily more tightly integrated than traditional monolithic applications. If possible at all, the latter can only be integrated via untyped low-level ser-

vices such as serial byte streams; e.g., via Unix pipes. If components interact closely via high-level data structures (objects), this raises the concern for the robustness of a solution based on components. An integrated system is only as robust as its least reliable component. In particular, there should be an attempt to limit the effects of a malfunctioning component to itself, e.g., it should still be possible to save a document that contains a crashed part. Such a bug-containment is impossible if a component can violate basic assumptions on which other components rely.

In particular, one type of error is notorious in this regard: memory management errors, such as dangling pointers and memory leaks. Oberon solves this problem by relying on automatic garbage collection. Garbage collection guarantees the correct handling of memory allocation.

In general, software safety is understood as the ability of a system to guarantee invariants at a particular abstraction level. For example, a garbage collector guarantees memory invariants at the programming-language level. It would be desirable if components could be protected at the hardware level. Unfortunately, current hardware-protection facilities are ill suited for components, since they imply a separation of components into different address spaces. Since communication across address spaces is expensive, this makes it impossible to be safe and efficient at the same time. This leads to less than satisfying tradeoffs.

For example, OpenDoc uses a separate address space for each document, but affords no protection inside a document. The strong static encapsulation properties of Oberon modules allow one to achieve a similar degree of protection without hardware assistance. They statically prevent violations of many invariants by code residing in other modules.

Furthermore, Oberon/F consequently prevents errors from propagating beyond their sources by applying precondition checks on procedure entry, i.e., by programming defensively. Components typically consist of many related classes. These classes must be able to interact in more flexible ways than with unrelated classes, e.g., clients of their abstraction.

For example, a file access path must be kept consistent with its file descriptor, otherwise arbitrary disk errors could be produced. In such a case, a private interface is needed between the file descriptor and file access path objects. Since information hiding in Oberon occurs on the module level, exported items in one module have complete access to each other's implementation details, which allows private interactions that cannot be disturbed by other modules. From a safety perspective, modules as information-hiding boundaries are important because they allow one to guarantee cross-class invariants [Szype92].

Multiplatform Support

Platform independence was one of the most important design goals for Oberon/F. Personal computers and workstations are the main targets for Oberon/F implementations, although the non-interactive parts could also be implemented on pure server machines, e.g., to form application servers in a three-tiered client/server model. Portability is achieved at the source-code level, since the Oberon/F programming interfaces are completely portable. Documents are stored in a portable binary format. Differences between platforms, e.g., between the OLE and OpenDoc user interfaces, are encapsulated into services that are provided as blackboxes by Oberon/F itself, so that clients automatically take on the correct look-and-feel.

User interface details are largely hidden from a programmer. For example, there are no public interfaces for the handling of windows or menus. Instead, suitable abstract property messages are defined, e.g., for inquiring or setting the font attributes of a selection, independ-

dent of whether there exists a separate font menu (Macintosh) or not (Windows).

Conclusions

Designing Oberon/F was an exercise in balancing different and often conflicting goals. One particularly relevant balancing act was between isolation and integration. Features that are completely isolated from each other are independent. This has the tremendous advantage that they can be designed, implemented, documented, comprehended, and modified without affecting each other.

With every large software project, a philosophy of "divide and conquer" is necessary in order to keep complexity under control and establish safety properties. On the other hand, the power of component software comes from integration.

Integrating independently developed components is the key to software whose power grows exponentially, while its size grows linearly. Each new component adds additional leverage to some or all of the already existing components. Integration patterns can be complex. They introduce mutual dependencies, and ripple effects if one component is modified.

This price must be paid; the art lies in minimizing it. In order to achieve a good balance, Oberon/F has gone through many design iterations. With each iteration, new requirements have been supported. New requirements have been derived, e.g., by implementing new document parts.

Currently, there exists a multitude of Oberon/F parts, many of which can cooperate in non-trivial ways. The support for OLE and OpenDoc guarantees a steady supply of additional components, and prevents Oberon/F from becoming an automation island. The consequent use of Oberon enables the rapid creation and assembly of components that are portable, efficient, and robust.

References

[Brock95] Brockschmidt, K., *Inside OLE2*, Microsoft Press, 1994.

[Cotte95] Cotter, S. and Potel, M., *Inside Taligent Technology*, Addison-Wesley, 1995.

[Deuts89] Deutsch, P., *Design Reuse and Frameworks in the Smalltalk-80 System Software Reusability, Vol 2*, Biggerstaff, T.J. and Perlis, A.J., Eds., ACM Press, 1989.

[Gosli96] Gosling, J., Joy, B., and Steele, G., *The Java Language Specification*, Addison-Wesley, 1996.

[Johns94] Johnson, R., *How to Design Frameworks Tutorial Notes of Object Technology at Work*, University of Zurich, 1994.

[Krasn88] Krasner, G. Pope, S., A Cookbook for Using the MVC User Interface Paradigm in Smalltalk, *Journal of Object-Oriented Programming*, Aug/Sep 88.

[MacAp96] Lewis, T., Ed., *Object-Oriented Application Frameworks*, Manning, 1995.

[ODF96] **http://www.devtools.apple.com/odf/index.html**

[OM96] **http://www.oberon.ch/customers/omi**

[OpenD96] Feiler, J. and Meadow, A., *Essential OpenDoc*, Addison-Wesley, 1996.

[Reise92] Reiser, M., Wirth, N., *Programming in Oberon—Steps beyond Pascal and Modula-2*, Addison-Wesley, 1992.

[Szype92] Szyperski, C., Import is not Inheritance—Why we need both: Modules and Classes, *Proceedings, 6th European Conf. on Object-Oriented Programming Lecture Notes in Computer Science 615*, 19–32, June 92.

[Visua92] Visual Basic Microsoft, Seattle, 1992.

[Willi94] Williams, S. and Kindel, C., The component object model, *Dr. Dobb's Special Report*, Winter 1994/95.

Dr. Cuno Pfister is with Oberon Microsystems, Inc., Technoparkstrasse 1 CH-8005, Zürich, Switzerland. Phone: (+411) 445 1751. Fax: (+411) 445 1752. Email: pfister@oberon.ch.

Associate Prof. Dr. Clemens Szyperski is Director, Programming Languages and Systems, Research School of Computing Science, Queensland University of Technology, Brisbane Q 4001, Australia. Phone: (+617) 3864 2132. Fax: (+617) 3864 1801. Email: c.szyperski@qut.edu.au

Let's Brew Some Java

Jose De Jesus

Introduction

Java is a platform-independent, object-oriented programming language designed by Sun Microsystems for network computing. The language includes features for writing stand-alone applications, applets (classes that enhance web pages), protocol handlers (like http, ftp, and telnet), and MIME content handlers (like video/mpeg, application/tiff, and image/jpeg). Java is currently available for SPARC Solaris, OS/2 Warp, AIX, System 7, Windows NT, Windows 95, and Windows 3.1.

Design

British scientist C.A.R. Hoare once advised an audience of computer designers to seek "consolidation, not innovation" when designing a new language. The inventors of Java followed this dictum by not creating an entirely new language, but rather by consolidating parts of C++ with extensions (i.e., interfaces) from Objective C. However, they eliminated some of C++'s more difficult features to make Java simpler, safer, and more portable. Java's major characteristics include:

Platform Independence
Instead of an executable module, the Java compiler produces a .class file that contains bytecodes for the Java Virtual Machine—a software abstraction of a real computer. Bytecodes include one-byte operation codes (opcodes) and optional operands to complete an instruction. Many instructions do not have operands. At runtime, the Java interpreter translates bytecodes into real code for the underlying computer. Thus, a .class file is architecture-neutral; it can run without changes or recompilation on any Java platform.

Compactness
The Java Virtual Machine is only 64K, making it possible for small electronic devices (i.e., specialized cellular phones) to run applets.

Simplicity, Safety, and Better Portability
Java's syntax is almost identical to C++ syntax, but the language is easier to learn because it uses a simpler object-oriented programming model, and eliminates many of the difficulties encountered with C++. Java is also a safe system because the Java Virtual Machine does not trust the contents of the .class file, but rather verifies bytecodes before executing them. In general, the Java language features:

- A simpler object oriented programming model

- No support for operator overloading

- Single inheritance (multiple inheritance is accomplished through interfaces—a concept borrowed from Objective C)

- No support for preprocessor, pointers, or goto statements

- No structs or unions

- No support for procedural programming (i.e., functions)

- Built-in threads, monitors, and automatic garbage collection

The following conditions also apply:

- Data types have fixed (not platform-dependent) sizes.

- Boolean variables cannot be coerced to integers; they are always either true or false, not 1 or 0.

- Unlike C and C++, Java defines how to handle operator side effects, so expressions can produce the same result across platforms.

- Java is stack-oriented, which makes it easier to type check.

- Java provides support for the Unicode Character Set—a 16-bit character-encoding system that supports the symbols of the principal written languages of the world.

Java Language Elements

Except for minor differences, Java is similar in lexical structure and grammar to C++.

Tokens
Tokens are the smallest meaningful units in a programming language. Java tokens include keywords, identifiers, literals, operators, and separators. Separators include whitespace and comments.

Whitespace
The Java whitespace characters include: Space, Horizontal Tab, Formfeed, Carriage Return, Linefeed, Carriage Return + Linefeed. The ASCII SUB(Ctrl+Z) character is also a white space when it is the last token in a program. For Java, a Carriage Return, a Linefeed, or a carriage return directly followed by a Linefeed character is a Line Terminator.

Table 1. Java Keywords

abstract	default	if	outer	this
boolean	do	implements	package	throw
break	double	import	private	throws
byte	else	inner	protected	transient
byvalue	extends	instanceof	public	try
case	final	int	rest	var
cast	finally	interface	return	void
catch	float	long	short	volatile
char	for	native	static	while
class	future	new	super	
const	generic	null	switch	
continue	goto	operator	synchronized	

Comments

Java supports three types of comments:

```
/* Traditional C-style comment */
// A C++ style comment
/** Documentation comment */
```

The first line denotes a C-style. Like C, Java ignores all text between /* and */. The double-slash, adopted from C++, makes a comment out of the rest of a line. And the /** and */ combination lets you create HTML documentation for programs using the Document Generator (javadoc).

Keywords

Some Java 1.0 keywords are listed in Table 1. Java 1.0 does not support goto statements. Instead, Java programmers use labels with the keywords break and continue used mostly to exit out of nested loops. Other reserved words that Java 1.0 does not support include: byvalue, cast, const, future, generic, inner, operator, outer, rest, and var.

Identifiers

Java identifiers can start with a letter, an underscore mark, or a dollar sign. Except for the first character, an identifier can also contain digits and Unicode characters above the hexadecimal number \00C0. THe length of Java identifiers is unlimited.

Literals

Java supports literals of type integer, floating point, boolean, character, and string.

Integer literals may be represented in decimal (10), hexadecimal (0xA), or octal (012) form.

Floating point values can be of type float (32-bit single precision) or double (64-bit double precision). Operations on them follow the ANSI/IEEE 754-1985 Standard for Binary Floating-Point Arithmetic.

Boolean literals are either true or false, and cannot be represented with integers (i.e., zero does not mean false, and non-zero does not mean true).

Character literals are of type char, and belong to the Unicode character set. They can be single characters or escape sequences, enclosed in single quotes.

String literals consist of zero or more characters enclosed in double quotes.

Operators

Java supports the following operators (some rules apply to arithmetic expressions):

- Operations on integers never return a result of type char, short, or byte. For example, if a variable x is declared byte, $x + 2$ would still return an int.

- If one of the operands is of type long, the result is also long.

- An expression produces a double-precision value if at least one of the operands is of double-precision. In general, if the operands are of the same type, the result will also be of that type.

- If the operands have different types, Java will coerce the operands to their common type.

See Table 2 for a list of arithmetic operators and Table 3 for a list of logical/bitwise operators.

Types

Java's basic or scalar data types include integer (byte, short, int, long), floating point (float, double), character, and boolean. Java's non-scalar types include arrays, classes, and interfaces. Arrays are dynamically allocated objects rather than C-like types. Therefore, an array operation is done through the array's methods.

Table 2. Arithmetic Operators

Type	Operator	Operation
Unary	-	negation
	~	one's complement
	++	increment
	--	decrement
Binary	=	assignment
	+	addition/concatenation
	+=	addition
	-	subtraction
	-=	subtraction
	*	multiplication
	*=	multiplication
	/	division
	/=	division
	%	modulo
	%=	modulo
	>>	right shift
	>>=	right shift (propagate sign)
	>>>	zero-fill right shift
	<<	left shift

Like C++, Java supports encapsulation, inheritance, and polymorphism, through the use of classes. However, unlike C++, Java does not support multiple inheritance. Instead, Java provides interfaces that allow objects to support common behaviors without sharing any implementation.

Statements

Java statements work in a manner similar to C/C++ statements. They include:

```
Empty:
```
An empty statement does nothing.

```
Labeled
exit: Sys-
tem.out.println("\n\nGoodbye!");
```

```
Expression
  Assignments:X = 1;
  PreIncrement:++X;
  PostIncrement:X++;
  PreDecrement:--X;
  PostDecrement:X--;
```

Table 3. Logical/Bitwise Operators

Types	Operator	Operation
Unary	!	negation
	&&	logical AND
	||	logical OR
Binary	&	bitwise AND
	&=	bitwise AND update
	|	bitwise OR
	|=	bitwise OR update
	^	bitwise XOR
	^=	bitwise XOR update
	>	greater than
	<	less than
	>=	greater than or equal to
	<=	less than or equal to
	==	equal to
	!=	not equal to
ternary	?:	if, then

```
MethodCall:X = GetValue();
AllocationExpression:byte[][] A
   = new byte[3][7];
```

Selection:
Java's selection (conditional) statements include if and switch constructs:
```
/* if construct */
if (expression)
  statement1
  [else statement2]
  /* switch construct */
  switch (expression)
{
  case expression: statement;
  case expression: statement;
  ...
  [default: statement;]
}
```

Iteration:
Iteration statements include for, while, and do-while:
```
/* for loop */
for ( initialization; [expression];
[increment])
statement;
/* while loop */
while (expression)
statement;
/* do-while loop */
do
  statement
  while expression;
```

Jump:
The jump statements (break, continue, return, and throw) transfer control unconditionally:
```
break [label]
```

```
continue [labe]
return [expression]
throw expression
```

Break and `continue` are used to exit out of loops.

Return is used to jump to a calling statement, optionally returning a value, and `throw` is used to throw (cause) an exception.

`Synchronization:`
Each class or object has a lock that it can use to synchronize sections of code to keep them from executing at the same time. The keyword synchronized marks a block of code as critical, and does not allow any other code to execute while the synchronized code is running:

```
    synchronized (expression)
{
    critical code
}
```

`Exception:`
Exception statements involve the keywords try, catch, and finally. Try tests the code that might throw an exception, while catch attempts to match and handle the thrown exception. Finally allows you to add code that should execute whether or not the exception is thrown:

```
try
  {
    /* code that might throw an ex-
      ception */
  }
catch (exceptiontype exceptionname)
  {
    /* exception-handling code */
  }
finally
  {
    /* this code executes anyway */
  }
```

Conclusion

The World Wide Web has provided the infrastructure for people everywhere to access hypertext documents. Java allows us to make this content interactive (in the form of applets). The Java phenomenon is changing our way of distributing and sharing software. Combined with other technologies such as OpenDoc and DSOM, Java can become a major player in our ever-shrinking world!

Jose De Jesus has worked with the Internet and OOP languages for over seven years. He is the author of *Borland Pascal With Objects 7.0,* published in 1993 by MIS:Press. His Java tutorials on the World Wide Web have attracted thousands of readers, gaining him an excellent reputation for presenting complex topics in simple ways.

Specification and Implementation of CORBAservices
A Case Study—Extended Abstract

Bernhard Hollunder
hollunder@io.freinet.de

While the specification of an Object Request Broker (ORB) defines basic functions for the transparent invocation of requests in a heterogeneous distributed environment [OMG95a], the so-called CORBAservices specify further sets of fundamental services that greatly facilitate the realization of distributed systems. The deployment of the standard operations provided by the CORBAservices not only simplifies the development of large scale systems, but also enables the building of programs that are easily *portable* between the ORB implementations of different vendors. Thus, it seems feasible to build *"ORB-portable" programs*, i.e., programs that can be compiled and executed with only slight or even with no modification using different ORB implementations. However, this approach is viable only if the available ORB implementations realize the CORBAservices completely and according to the required specification.

In this paper we investigate to what extent the currently available ORB implementations provide the operations of the CORBA-services. Unfortunately, most of the ORB implementations that provide (some of) the CORBAservices, such as DSOM from IBM, ORB Plus from HP, and Orbix from Iona, are still in beta testing. Currently available ORB releases comprising several CORBAservices are HP's Distributed Smalltalk and Sun's NEO.

We will not discuss here each of the ten CORBAservices that have already been specified by the Object Management Group (for a description of eight of these service see [OMG95b]). Instead, we restrict our attention to one specific service, the *event management* service. The reason for choosing this service is, on the one hand, that it introduces important capabilities for asynchronous communication between objects (recall that a standard CORBA request results in a synchronous execution of the operation), while on the other hand, the event management service is not too complex to be discussed here.

The *event management* service is based on the notions of supplier and consumer. A *supplier* is an object that produces event data, while a *consumer* is an object that processes event data. Depending on whether a supplier or a consumer initiates the event communication, we distinguish two models: the push model and the pull model. In the *push* model the supplier initiates the transfer of event data by invoking the operation push provided by the consumer. In the *pull* model the consumer requests event data from the supplier by using the operation pull provided by the supplier. Both the push and pull function are supplied with a single parameter of type CORBA::Any that packages all the event data.

There is no direct communication between suppliers and consumers; instead so-called *event channels* serve as intervening objects. Event channels allow multiple suppliers to communicate with multiple consumers asynchronously. Since an event channel on the one hand receives event data from suppliers and on the other hand passes event data to the registered consumers, an event channel thus adopts the role of both a supplier and a consumer object. Event channels are standard CORBA objects, which means that the communication with an event channel is accomplished using standard CORBA requests.

The operations of the *event management* service (as well as of the other CORBAservices) are completely described in OMG's Interface Definition Language (IDL). The *event management* service introduces the following three modules: CosEventComm, CosEventChannel-Admin, and CosTypedEventChannelAdmin. The CosEventComm module introduces generic operations both for initiating event communication and for disconnecting suppliers and consumers from an event channel. These operations are inherited by the other two modules. While the CosEventChannelAdmin module allows the creation and handling of untyped event channels (i.e., the event data transmitted are of the type CORBA::Any), the CosTypedEventChannelAdmin can be used to establish typed communication between suppliers and consumers. This means that suppliers and consumers can use the operations of some mutually agreed-upon interface.

Having described the structure and the basic functions of the *event management* service, let us now turn our attention to its realization. Currently, the following ORB implementations support the *event management* service: NEO, Distributed Smalltalk; DSOM (beta), ORB Plus (beta), and Orbix (beta). In the following discussion, we concentrate on NEO's event management service.[1]

Basically, the NEO system only partially implements the functions of the *event management* service. To be more precise, we can distinguish the following three cases:

- The module CosEventComm is realized as specified by the CORBAservices.

---

1. As soon as other ORB implementations provide the event management services they will, of course, be included in the following discussion. Please contact me (preferably per e-mail) to obtain the most recent version of this paper.

- Almost all operations of the module CosEventChannelAdmin are supported; however, the CosEventChannelAdmin has a different internal structure as different names are employed as well.

- NEO does not implement the module CosTypedEventChannelAdmin.

In addition, NEO's event management service provides a further kind of event channel, so-called indexed event channels. In contrast to the aforementioned channels, an indexed event channel never discards events until explicitly requested.

The following table summarizes the availability of the *event management* service:

	CORBA-services	NEO
Basic functions	+	+
Untyped event channel	+	(+)
Typed event channel	+	-
Indexed event channel	-	+

+ Available

- Not available

(+) The functionality is available; however the respective interfaces are organized differently

To sum up, NEO currently shares only a restricted set of functions that are implemented as required by the CORBAservice specification. This is not surprising, as the standard is slowly (but surely) becoming a reality. However, this means that it will take some time until the available ORBs (in particular NEO) have been adapted.

Interestingly, the Gartner Group summarizes their point of view as follows: *"Finally, we do not believe vendors want compatibility enough to comply with detailed standards. As such, OMG will never make competing ORBs 100 percent compatible, although it probably will make ORBs more compatible than they would have been if CORBA did not exist."* [Gartn95, p. 46].

Consequently, to develop today (and even in the near future) ORB-portable programs that exploit, for example, *event management* functionalities, only those functions should be deployed that are commonly available by different ORB implementations. This, however, means that the application programmer currently cannot exploit the full power of the CORBAservices.

To mitigate the current tradeoffs, therefore, we propose a *Framework Component* approach: Given a function of the event management service (or, in general, of some CORBAservice), the Framework Component maps it, depending on a particular ORB, to a function that is provided by the ORB in question. Hence, the application programmer can use the functions as specified by the CORBAservice, and it is the Framework Component's part to bridge the gap between the specification and the implementation of the CORBAservices.

The mapping comes in different flavors: If, for example, an ORB provides implementations of all functions introduced by the CORBA-

service, the mapping is rather trivial. On the other extreme, if the ORB does not implement any CORBAservice, the mapping itself has to implement the function by using only low-level functions. The currently available CORBA-service implementations (in particular, NEO) are in between both extremes (as exemplified above by the event management service).

References

[Gartn95] The Gartner Group, Three-Tier Computing Architectures and Beyond, *Strategic Analysis Report,* 1995.

[OMG95a] The Object Management Group, *The Common Object Request Broker: Architecture and Specification,* Revision 2.0, 1995.

[OMG95b] The Object Management Group, *CORBAservices: Common Object Services Specification,* Revised Edition, OMG Document Number 95-3-31, 1995.

Interactive Objects Software GmbH, Basler Straße 63, D-79100 Freiburg, Germany, Tel.: [+49] 761 / 400730, email: hollunder@io.freinet.de

GINA

An Object-Oriented Run-Time and Development Solution for Distributed Object Computing

Sverker Norrefeldt
Sverker.Norrefeldt@mch.sni.de

The solution GINA (General Interface for Network Applications) offers a framework for the implementation and operation of object-oriented transaction-based client-server applications.

Siemens Nixdorf's (SNI) GINA API is an object-oriented solution for heterogeneous, distributed applications that are designed for On-Line Transaction Processing (OLTP) operations and rightsizing of mainframe-based systems to more decentralized transaction processing operations.

GINA offers the following functionality:

- Transaction-based communication of distributed objects

- Transaction-based storage of persistency objects

- Transparent access to persistent and transient objects

- Complete embedding in C++ (inheritance, polymorphism, etc.)

- Connectivity to heterogeneous OLTP systems

- Recovery for distributed transactions

- Support functions for use in distributed environments

GINA Components

GINA contains the following components:

- *T-ORB.* The transaction-based object request broker offers safe communi-

cations paths between objects across platforms.

- *Persistency Service.* The persistency service defines a framework for persistent storage of object networks. The APIs have been modeled on the Object Database Standard ODMG-93.

- *Support.* This component connects T-ORB and Persistency Service. It integrates distributed applications.

GINA Development System

GINA supports the paradigm for object-oriented programming with C++, including inheritance and polymorphism. The development system offers the following tools:

- *Generator for the persistency service.* The generator helps you to map the C++ object model into relations for an RDBMS and to create the necessary methods accessing the database.

- *Schema Development Generator.* This generator offers the ability to change the object model for an existing database without having to recreate the database (available with GINA release 2.0).

- *CORBA IDL Compiler.* The IDL compiler generates the local client stub and the remote server interface from CORBA IDL definitions (available with GINA release 2.0).

- *Interface Generator.* The interface generator analyses the C++ object model and generates the remote client stub and the remote interface to the server (available with GINA release 2.0).

- *Machine-Independent Object Generator.* Analyses the C++ object model and generates source files for encoding and decoding T-ORB messages (available with GINA release 2.0).

GINA Runtime System
GINA is based on tried, proven, and trusted technologies. Currently, the following products are used:

- openUTM (transaction processing monitor)
- INFORMIX-Online (RDBMS)

GINA is available for:

- SINIX V5.42
- Sun Solaris V2.4 / V2.5
- HP-UX V9.05 / V10
- Windows-NT V3.51 (available with GINA release 2.0)

The GINA runtime system contains:

- Runtime libraries for T-ORB, Persistency Service and Support

- Configuration Tool. The configuration tool takes a description of the intended T-ORB runtime environment for a distributed system and generates configuration files for the necessary components.

GINA History
GINA was originally created as a project-specific solution for a large TMN system

commissioned by Deutsche Telekom AG (German Telecom). It was designed for operation in real-world, heterogeneous, distributed and object-oriented applications. The first GINA prototype was released in early 1995. GINA release 1.0 was issued in September 1995, and it is used as an object-oriented platform for TMN applications by Deutsche Telekom AG.

GINA—Domain of Application
The following requirements may lead you to use GINA:

- The system should be a object-oriented client-server system

- There are strong demands on data consistency

- Gradual migration of mainframe OLTP applications

- It must be possible to connect the system to other applications (LU6.x, OSI-TP)

- The system must be available today

Contact

Please do not hesitate to contact us if you would like to have more information about GINA. Direct you inquiries to:
Sverker Norrefeldt
SNI GP NM TK3
Otto-Hahn Ring 6 D-81730
Munich, Germany
Phone: +49 89 636 49735
Fax: +49 89 636 48303
Email: **Sverker.Norrefeldt@mch.sni.de**